THE CRITICS DEBATE

General Editor Michael Scott

The Critics Debate
General Editor Michael Scott
Published titles:
Sons and Lovers Geoffrey Harvey
Bleak House Jeremy Hawthorn
The Canterbury Tales Alcuin Blamires
Tess of the d'Urbervilles Terence Wright

Further titles are in preparation.

BLEAK HOUSE

Jeremy Hawthorn

MACMILLAN

For my wife, Bjørg

First published 1987

Published by
Higher and Further Education Division
MACMILLAN PUBLISHERS LTD
Houndmills, Basingstoke, Hampshire RG21 2XS
and London
Companies and representatives
throughout the world

Printed in Hong Kong

Hawthorn, Jeremy
Charles Dickens, Bleak House. – (The Critics Debate)
1. Dickens, Charles, *1812-1870*. Bleak House
I. Title II. Series
823′.8 PR4556

ISBN 0–333–37866–0
ISBN 0–333–37867–9 Pbk

Contents

Part Two: Appraisal 50

General Editor's Preface

OVER THE last few years the practice of literary criticism has become hotly debated. Methods developed earlier in the century and before have been attacked and the word 'crisis' has been drawn upon to describe the present condition of English Studies. That such a debate is taking place is a sign of the subject discipline's health. Some would hold that the situation necessitates a radical alternative approach which naturally implies a 'crisis situation'. Others would respond that to employ such terms is to precipitate or construct a false position. The debate continues but it is not the first. 'New Criticism' acquired its title because it attempted something fresh calling into question certain practices of the past. Yet the practices it attacked were not entirely lost or negated by the new critics. One factor becomes clear: English Studies is a pluralistic discipline.

What are students coming to advanced work in English for the first time to make of all this debate and controversy? They are in danger of being overwhelmed by the cross curents of critical approached as they take up their study of literature. The purpose of this series is to help delineate various critical approaches to specific literary texts. Its authors are from a variety of critical schools and have approached their task in a flexible manner. Their aim is to help the reader come to terms with the variety of criticism and to introduce him or her to further reading on the subject and to a fuller evaluation of a particular text by illustrating the way it has been approached in a number of contexts. In the first part of the book a critical survey is given of some of the major ways the text has been appraised. This is done sometimes in a thematic manner, sometimes according to various 'schools' or 'approaches'. In the second part the authors provide their own appraisals of the text from their stated critical standpoint, allowing the reader the knowledge of their own particular approaches from which their views may in turn be evaluated. The series therein hopes to introduce and to elucidate criticism of authors and texts being studied and to encourage participation as the critics debate.

Michael Scott

A Note on Text and References

I HAVE throughout used the Penguin edition of *Bleak House*, edited by Norman Page and with an Introduction by J. Hillis Miller (1971). Page references to the novel in the subsequent discussion are to this edition. Other works cited are identified by author and date of first publication, with page references as appropriate; full details of the works in question will be found in the References. Repeated references to the same work are by page number only.

There are variants between different texts of the novel available, and the reader should perhaps know a little about the debates concerning these. *Bleak House* was first published in nineteen monthly parts, of which the final part was a 'double number', from March 1852 to September 1853. It was published in book form in 1853, and subsequently in a number of different editions. The Penguin text is based on the 1868 Charles Dickens Edition, and the Penguin editor defends this choice by claiming that this was the edition which incorporates Dickens's final revisions.

His position has been (implicitly) attacked by the editors of the Norton Critical Edition of *Bleak House* (1977), George Ford and Sylvère Monod. They claim that there is 'very little evidence' that Dickens revised the text of *Bleak House* for the Charles Dickens Edition, and they argue very strongly in favour of their choice of the first, 1853, edition of the novel as 'copy text' for their edition.

My own opinion is that their argument is correct. I have however chosen to use the Penguin edition of the novel for purposes of reference, as (i) it is very widely used, (ii) it is cheaper than the Norton Critical Edition, and (iii) it does not reprint the text of the Charles Dickens Edition unchanged, but uses, on occasions, readings from the 1853 edition. I have confirmed that none of my references or critical arguments involves the use of what is possibly a passage of dubious textual authority in the Penguin edition.

As I have tried to give a good indication of where in a particular chapter passages to which I am referring occur, in addition to the Penguin-edition page reference, readers who prefer to use the Norton Critical Edition should be able to trace references without too much difficulty. The Norton Critical Edition includes a list of textual variants which readers of the novel will find of great interest.

Introduction

ACCORDING to G.K. Chesterton – an early and influential critic of Dickens – there is no such novel as *Nicholas Nickleby*, no such novel as *Our Mutual Friend:* they are 'simply lengths cut from the flowing and mixed substance called Dickens' (1906, p.66).

It isn't hard to see what Chesterton is getting at: Dickens's novels all share family resemblances, and, as many subsequent critics have pointed out with varying degrees of approval, they all make us think about Dickens the man. But it is very dangerous to exaggerate as Chesterton does and to suggest that Dickens's novels possess no distinct individuality, to imply that one novel is merely a continuation of its predecessor. A novel from Dickens's later period such as *Bleak House* is not only very different from an early work such as *The Pickwick Papers;* it is also sharply different in many ways from *David Copperfield* and *Hard Times* – the two novels of Dickens's which, respectively, preceded and followed *Bleak House.*

Recent criticism has given *Bleak House* a higher and higher placing amongst Dickens's major novels, and to a considerable extent this is because its unique qualities and distinctive identity have been more and more carefully observed. This historical process of coming to terms with the individual greatness of *Bleak House* is one of the reasons why my Survey of critical treatments of the novel tries to maintain a sense of historical perspective, to show how critical views of the novel have changed over time. It is also the case that the more we are able to set critical accounts of a work in a historical context the more likely we are to be able to consider to what extent our own critical responses to a work are historically conditioned or limited.

With one exception I have not divided my Survey of critical treatments of *Bleak House* according to literary-critical 'schools' or 'approaches'. This is because the comprehensiveness of Dickens's vision seems to discourage narrowly doctrinaire treatments of his works. Indeed, some of the most interesting criticism of *Bleak House* has involved debate between critics of very varying persuasions about key aspects of the novel: its portrayal and analysis of Victorian society, its narrative structure and technique, and its characters. My one exception here is the consideration of feminist views of the novel in my third section. (Many of the critics I refer to in this section are actually male, but their criticism of *Bleak House* is, nevertheless, not inaccurately described as 'feminist' in many cases.)

Along with other of Dickens's later novels, *Bleak House* involves proportionately less *celebration* of life and proportionately more *analysis* of and *commentary* on it. This is the justification for spending so much time talking about relatively serious matters such as the portrayal of Victorian society and the analysis of the family and of sexuality in the novel. But for the ordinary reader of *Bleak House* (and even, let us hope, for the academic reader) the novel provides, along with such serious possibilities, excitement, tension, amusement and imaginative challenge. In my concluding Appraisal, therefore, I have tried both to give my own view on the critical debates I have outlined in the Survey part of this book, and also to get as close as possible to the actual reading-experiences that *Bleak House* can provide.

I hope that the reader will be tolerant of the fact that my chosen structure necessarily involves a certain amount of repetition. Rather than dealing with one critic's opinion once, as would be possible were the book to have been structured according to different critical schools or approaches, I have often had to refer to the same critical book or essay on a number of different occasions. I have tried not to repeat myself too much, and often, of course, one can draw attention to rather different points of significance in the same critical account of the novel or an aspect of the novel.

The reader should know something of my own critical position. My personal bias is towards seeing literary works – and critical treatments of them – in their social and historical contexts, and if I were forced to characterise my position very simply then I would call myself a Marxist critic. But, as I argue later on in this book, Marxist criticism has developed very considerably in the four and a half decades which have elapsed since the first Marxist study of Dickens was published. To be a Marxist critic is certainly *not* to feel the need to reject all non-Marxist critical accounts of *Bleak House*, and I hope that my final Appraisal of the novel and of the critical treatments it has received will strike no one as narrowly doctrinaire or prejudiced.

PART ONE: SURVEY

The anatomy of society

THE argument that a literary work is in some way 'about' the society to which its author belonged has generally been a somewhat controversial literary-critical standpoint in the present century. It has often been particularly associated with Marxist or sociological critical approaches, which have attempted to demonstrate that literary works 'reflect' society in some way or another, and such approaches have often been criticised for claiming too simple a relationship between literature and society, too narrow a view of the value of literary art, and too low an estimation of the individual contribution made by an author to his or her work.

'Bleak House' and Victorian England

In the case of *Bleak House,* however, critics belonging to almost every possible 'school' or approach have agreed that *Bleak House* makes its readers think about Victorian society, and that Dickens clearly intended that this should be the case. When, at the end of chapter 47 of the novel, we read the rhetorical address to 'your Majesty', 'my lords and gentlemen', 'Right Reverends and Wrong Reverends of every order', and 'men and women, born with Heavenly compassion in your hearts', telling them all that Jo is dead, and concluding with the words, 'And dying thus around us every day', it is difficult to feel that these are purely imaginary personages who are called upon to think about merely fictional events. 'Us' refers to Dickens's contemporary readers; those who are 'dying thus around' them are real, living counterparts to the fictional Jo.

But if there is some critical consensus that *Bleak House* is in some way 'about' Victorian society, there are still very important disagreements about the *nature*, and the *importance* of this social concern. Dickens's early readers and critics saw him very much as a *reformer* – in other words, as one engaged in the attempt to counter very specific abuses and wrongs. Many of the early reviews of *Bleak House* which are conveniently reprinted in the *Casebook* on the novel edited by A.E. Dyson (1969 a) show that this was very much how Dickens's contemporaries saw the novel's social significance. The October 1853 review in *Bentley's Monthly Review*, for example, after some largely descriptive comments on plot and character, continues, 'But . . . Mr Dickens always writes *with a purpose* now. And what is the task he has set before him in *Bleak House?* No less a one than the exposure of the infamies of Chancery' (Dyson, 1969 a, p.69). It then goes on to find fault with Dickens's knowledge of the legal system, something which a number of later commentators have also done. W.P. Williams (1944), for example, pointed out that Chancery would not have been called upon to adjudicate between a number of rival wills; this would have been a matter for a Probate judge.

Generations of ordinary readers have not been too worried by such niceties. Listening to a BBC radio programme broadcast in July 1984 on the free legal-aid system, I heard a disgruntled member of the public claim that things had changed very little since Dickens wrote *Bleak House*.

To suggest that *Bleak House* is in some sense an 'anatomy of society' is to go far beyond the argument that in the novel Dickens was concerned to attack specific abuses. First, it indicates that the novel is concerned to understand the nature and structure of a whole society, rather than to attack a few unsatisfactory parts. And, secondly, it implies that the primary importance of the novel resides in this anatomising of society. The term 'anatomy of society' comes from an influential and pioneering essay on Dickens by the American critic Edmund Wilson (1941). In this essay Wilson argues that by the mid 1840s Dickens had arrived at a point in his career at which he set out to trace an anatomy of society; *Dombey and Son* was his first attempt so to do, while *Bleak House* realised his intention to perfection.

For Wilson, everything in the novel contributes to this

central aim, not in the manner of an economist or a political theorist, but through the observed interrelations between highly individualised human beings. A.E. Dyson quotes an important passage from Wilson's essay in which Wilson argues for links between the fog at the start of chapter 1 of the novel, the legal institution of Chancery, and 'the whole web of clotted antiquated institutions in which England stifles and decays' (1969 a, p.16).

Wilson's view of *Bleak House* is representative of a dominant trend in modern critical responses to the novel. Edgar Johnson, Dickens's most respected recent biographer, claims in the Preface to his monumental study of the novelist that the unifying thread of Dickens's entire career was that of a critical analysis of modern society and its problems (1952, p.viii). Johnson sees *Bleak House* in particular *not* merely as an attack on a number of social abuses – the inefficient legal system, inadequate concern for the poor, insanitary conditions – but as an indictment of 'the whole dark muddle of organized society', with legal injustices not accidental but 'organically related to the very structure of that society' (Dyson, 1969 a, p.135). Early on in his biography Johnson quotes from a letter written by Dickens at the start of his literary career in July 1837, to the effect that fictitious narratives 'place the enormities of the system in a much stronger point of view' (1952, p.217). To critics such as Johnson and Wilson a later novel such as *Bleak House* manages to do this: to see abuses (enormities), but to set them in the context of a *system* – a total society.

Those recent critics who have agreed with this analysis of the novel's fundamental importance include – not surprisingly – Marxist critics as well as – perhaps surprisingly – critics concerned with formal and thematic aspects of *Bleak House*. The first significant Marxist study of Dickens was that by T.A. Jackson (1937), in which it was argued that the key to Dickens's work lay in his radicalism. Dickens's three major literary periods were related to three distinct historical periods in which radical views first had, then lost, political ascendancy and impetus. Jackson sees *Bleak House* as the most important of Dickens's works so far as the study of Dickens's views on the government of society are concerned, and he links the 'careful construction' of the novel with Dickens's social analysis. He finds it significant that *Bleak House*, unlike earlier novels of

Dickens's, lacks a single villain, and suggests that 'The villain whose villainy conditions the whole action, and in the end precipitates the culminating catastrophe, is The Law, and the actively-malevolent Vested Interest which it both protects and typifies' (p.134). According to Jackson's analysis of the novel, the greatness of *Bleak House* is directly related to its ability to expose the reality of Dickens's society. Not only is it critical of evangelical piety and of the Law, but it also shows how human beings were stunted and deformed by this society, and it is also radically critical of the bourgeois family (about which I will have more to say below).

Given the time at which it was written Jackson's analysis is a surprisingly sophisticated one, but it is not in essence remarkable that he should argue along the general lines that he does. It is more unusual to discover relatively 'formalist' critics (that is, critics concerned to examine literary works in terms more of their form than of their content, and in terms of their 'literary' rather than their 'social' qualities and meaning) also arguing that *Bleak House* is a novel that anatomises Victorian society.

J. Hillis Miller, for example, in his Introduction to the Penguin edition of *Bleak House*, argues that in writing the novel Dickens 'constructed a model in little of English society in his time' (1971, p.11), both because the novel accurately reflects the social reality of Dickens's day, but also because the network of relations among the various characters is a miniature version of the interconnectedness of people in all levels of society (pp. 11, 12). This double argument is itself representative of the way in which the 'anatomy of society' account of *Bleak House* has become more sophisticated in recent years, seeing the social analysis to take place on a number of different levels in the novel. The importance of disease in *Bleak House*, for example, has increasingly been treated in terms of its multiple, many-levelled significance by 'anatomy of society' critics. Of course Dickens was very concerned with the problem of contagious disease – indeed, in terms of his conscious intentions it is likely that his primary concern in introducing such illness into *Bleak House* was to campaign for those social reforms that would help to prevent the all-too-frequent epidemics from which the England of his day suffered. But many recent critics have also seen the symbolic force that disease assumes in *Bleak*

House: as Taylor Stoehr points out, the illness can be seen as a symbol of the secret and guilty connections between the high and low in society (1965, p.237). Andrew Sanders sees *Bleak House* as the most significant of Dickens's works which investigate the various effects of disease on urban life in the nineteenth century, but he further notes that 'an unspecified contagious disease', which is probably smallpox, becomes both a uniting image for the story and also 'a sign of the real destructiveness caused by the rottenness of society' (1982, p.6).

Many recent critics, then, have continued to see *Bleak House* in terms of its being an 'anatomy of society', but have analysed this anatomising in more and more subtle ways, stressing, in particular, the multi-levelled way in which the novel dissects Victorian society. In his recent book *Dickens: Novelist in the Market-Place*, James M. Brown comments directly upon this capacity of Dickens's works to refer analytically to society on a number of different levels simultaneously. He notes that a chapter in *Bleak House* can be a realistic description of the contemporary scene and, 'at the same time, without ever rendering this realistic meaning redundant, it can carry a figurative or representative significance of generalising importance to the world of the novel' (1982, p.9). He suggests that Chancery in *Bleak House* is, like the Circumlocution Office in *Little Dorrit*, a thing with its own life which is external to the individuals who have created it, and hence an appropriate symbol for mid-Victorian England. Moreover, he goes on to argue that the mature novels (including *Bleak House*) reflect not selected aspects of the surface of social life, 'but the *essential* condition of social relations within a *whole society*, which is seen as a social organism, a system of interrelated parts' (pp. 11, 14). Interestingly, he sees the depth of insight into the workings of society as a system in Dickens's novels to be far greater than the consciously held beliefs about Victorian society of either Dickens or any of his characters: according to Brown, at the same time that Dickens's own views were progressively hardening into conservative impatience with liberal opinion (in other words, at about the time that *Bleak House* was being written), his novels were revealing an increasingly challenging and critical social perspective. For Brown, Dickens's later novels (including *Bleak House*) show industrial society as an oppressive and alienating system which is external to the individuals within it and which turns these individuals into objects, machines or things. Brown thus takes a commonplace view of much previous criticism of Dickens, that in his novels the characteristics of living and non-living things are reversed; and gives it a specifically social significance: this is what Victorian society is like – it turns human beings into objects, and gives physical objects or abstract institutions human characteristics. This is not so far away from T.A. Jackson's suggestion that Dickens's novels contain caricatures because Victorian society turned real people into caricatures of themselves (1937, p.253).

Dissenting voices

Thus far I may well have suggested that, although there have been differences in the way critics have seen *Bleak House* as an anatomy of society, there has hardly been a *debate* about the central issue that it is with Victorian society, taken as a single complex system, that the novel is centrally concerned. But there have been important critical accounts of Dickens and of *Bleak House* which have fundamentally questioned this position. According to John Carey, for instance, we shall miss Dickens's real greatness if we persist in regarding him primarily as a critic of society (1973, p. 8). Carey does not dispute that this may well have been how Dickens saw himself, but he claims that Dickens's inability to take institutions seriously, and some of his more illiberal political attitudes, undercut his claim to be read as a critic of society. Carey notes that it is a characteristic of Dickens's mind that he can see almost everything from two (often, we might add, opposed) points of view, and that this makes him appear confused and hypocritical in his thinking about society. In *Bleak House* Carey recognises what the symbolism of the fog is aimed at – the legal system and characters' ignorance of one another – but he finds this symbolism to be crude and, in his words, 'best forgotten' (p. 112). For him Dickens is not good as a systematic thinker – and of course the analysis of a society requires systematic thought. Dickens's strength, Carey argues, is simile not symbolism, and his symbolic writing is best when it sticks closest to physical objects. It is Dickens's prodigal imagination, reaching typically into 'odd angles and side-alleys of his subject' (p. 7) that constitutes the essence of his greatness. Putting it simply: if we read *Bleak House* as an analysis of Victorian society we miss its greatness; Dickens is an inadequate social analyst, but a genius in the depiction of people and things peripheral to his social vision.

A very similar point is argued by another very influential critic of Dickens – George Orwell. According to Orwell Dickens may see human beings with intense vividness but he always sees them as 'characters' rather than as functional members of society. For Orwell the concreteness of Dickens's vision is a sign of what he misses: Dickens describes wonderfully an *appearance* but he does not often describe a *process* (1940, pp.441, 443). According to Orwell the outstanding, unmistakable mark of Dickens's writing is the 'unnecessary detail' (p.450) – a statement clearly closely related to Carey's argument that Dickens's genius is to be found in his treatment of his subject's odd angles and side-alleys.

Biography or social criticism?

A variant of this criticism is the argument that, in some way or another, the most important thing the reader of a Dickens novel obtains from it is not a knowledge of Dickens's society but some sort of knowledge of, or contact with, Dickens the man. Harvey Peter Sucksmith argues that Dickens's vision is largely an introverted one (1970, p.340), and Robert Garis, in a very influential study of Dickens, claims that Dickens was a 'theatrical' artist and that what we respond to in the novels is not the depicted real world but the performing artist. Of *Bleak House* in particular Garis argues that it starts Dickens's great campaign of indignant criticism of the world for failing to embody his own images of living and loving (1965, p.95), and, although he admits that Dickens's purpose in *Bleak House* is to demonstrate that the whole world (a significant expansion from Wilson's 'society') is penetrated, stifled and terrorised by a huge network of interconnecting systems, he finds Dickens's demonstration 'contrived'. We are given a large number of 'systematised characters', between whom many and varied interrelations are contrived, but Garis argues that Dickens is not really interested in how real people live their lives and that thus we enjoy watching him mimicking people without believing that what we are watching is actually taking place (p.105).

It is worth pointing out that Garis's position is diametrically opposed to that of many Dickens critics. John Forster, Dickens's friend and biographer, argued that no man ever had so surprising a faculty as Dickens of becoming himself what he was representing, and of entering into mental phases and processes so absolutely as to reproduce them completely in dialogue without the need of an explanatory word (1872–4, II, p.116). This is the opposite of the 'introverted vision' alleged of Dickens by Sucksmith.

We can sum up the foregoing disagreements by saying that the critics concerned agree that in *Bleak House* Dickens set out to anatomise his society or 'the world', but that this anatomising is either seen as powerful and the fundamental point of value in the novel, or it is seen as unsuccessful and peripheral to the novel's importance, which lies elsewhere.

A different sort of disagreement occurs when critics try to decide what *sort* of social analysis is to be found in *Bleak House*, and what Dickens's conclusions can be interpreted as after a reading of the novel. George Ford notes that an early reader of the novel, E.P. Whipple, reported that characters such as Vholes and Sir Leicester Dedlock delighted the liberals and angered the conservatives, whereas Mrs Jellyby delighted the conservatives and angered the liberals (1955, p.100).

We can contrast with the many confident accounts of *Bleak House* as anatomy of society the far more qualified view of George Orwell, who concedes that in every page that he wrote Dickens reveals a consciousness that society is wrong somewhere at the root, but who argues that Dickens's criticism of society is almost exclusively moral: Dickens, he claims, attacks such institutions as the law and parliamentary government without ever suggesting what he would replace them with. Orwell goes on to suggest that Dickens's target is not so much society as 'human nature': he never attacks the economic system *as a system*, nor does he ever attack private enterprise or private property (1940, p.416).

Victorian society or human nature?

This really leads us into a different aspect of the view that Dickens the novelist was primarily an anatomist of society and that *Bleak House* exemplifies this aspect of his genius most completely. Many critics have seen Dickens's subject in *Bleak House* to be far wider than Victorian society. Orwell's mention of 'human nature' chimes in with the earlier quoted comment of Robert Garis's about 'the world': in this view Dickens in *Bleak House* is attacking not the specific vices and shortcomings of one society but the human condition in general. J. Hillis Miller sees the novel's doomed law suit as symbolic not of the state of Victorian law so much as of life itself; he argues that to be involved in an endless case which can only be concluded by the total using-up of suit and suitor becomes a symbol in *Bleak House* of what it is to be in the world at all (1958, p.163). He makes pointed reference here to the irony of Richard Carstone's references to a 'final hearing' and a 'termination'. Other critics have commented on the large number of apocalyptic references in the novel – indeed, to the large number of biblical references in the work – and have suggested that these call to mind not one society but human life in general.

Mark Spilka, for example, says that the three orphans and their guardian are involved in a legal muddle which suggests Original Sin (1963, p.209). Q.D. Leavis, in one of the most important essays on *Bleak House*, implies that *both* the particular, social analysis *and* the larger, universal meanings can be found in the novel.

> It is not therefore the Law as such, but the laws of human nature and the society that man's nature has produced as the expression of our impulses, that constitute what John Jarndyce calls 'the family misfortune'. What rightly distresses Ada is the realization that merely by being born they are enemies in the struggle for existence – which the *laissez-faire* society of course did nothing to mitigate. (1970, p.131).

This interpretaion is very finely balanced between the particular (social) analysis and the more general (human) one, and Mrs Leavis goes on to see that litigation which is responsible for so much suffering in *Bleak House* as the essential characteristic of fallen mankind, the form that Original Sin may be said to take in the time of Dickens. She notes that Conversation Kenge in the novel describes the legal system as as old as old England itself (which, I would add, could be seen either as an indication that it represents something essentially human, or an indication that it represents something essentially English).

This same movement from particular social interpretations to more sombre and all-embracing views of *Bleak House*'s meaning can be seen in Dennis Walder's account of the novel in his recent book *Dickens and Religion*. Walder sees Dickens's pessimistic analysis of the social effects of contemporary religion in *Bleak House* as part of a more general indictment of institutions and their failure to minister to the real needs of individuals. He suggests that at times the Chancery case of Jarndyce and Jarndyce takes on the overtones of some primal curse upon mankind (1981, pp. 154, 155).

Symbol and image

This recurrent critical issue of 'either – or' versus 'both this and that' can be seen in critical treatments of many other aspects of the novel. Modern critics of all persuasions have been much influenced by those formalist critics (often referred to as New Critics) who demonstrated how techniques of analysis normally associated with poetry criticism could also very fruitfully be applied to novels. Recent critics have devoted ingenious attention to such matters as the use of recurrent images in *Bleak House*, Dickens's use of symbols in the novel, and the patterns of meaning detectable in such things as the biblical references in the work.

One of the most searching analyses of a particular 'family' of images in *Bleak House* is Norman Friedman's essay on 'sun' and 'shadow' references in the novel, an essay which also branches out into an investigation into other important images and symbols in the work. Given the importance of the city's growth in Victorian England, and the central place of London in Dickens's world in general and in *Bleak House* in particular, one might expect that sun–shadow images would be given a specifically social significance by Friedman. But he generally prefers to see them in a more universal way, talking about the novel's concern with 'the problem of evil' as mediated through its manipulation of such images, along with its stress on moral responsibility, a doctrine of 'secular sin and redemption' (1975, p.363). As Esther's name suggests, she is a 'summer sun' who disperses the shadow (just as John Carey argues that

Woodcourt, who we must perhaps assume 'would court' Esther given a little encouragement, disperses fog). But whether these complex webs of positive reference have a specifically *social* significance is a matter about which critics have disagreed. I shall talk more of Esther's 'meaning' in my next section; so far as Mrs Leavis is concerned, the fact that Woodcourt is a doctor is extremely important, as he represents a very positive set of values for Dickens through his profession (1970, p.152). I cannot resist quoting a rather embarrassing (for this viewpoint) comment from one of Dickens's letters on this subject: 'The longer I live, the more I doubt the doctors . . .' (Forster 1872–4, II, 54).

I have mentioned the crucial role of the city in Dickens's world and in Victorian England, and more than one critic has stressed the way in which Dickens took the city in general – or, more often, London in particular – as a model of Victorian society. Alexander Welsh in his *The City of Dickens* stresses the importance of the city in fostering Dickens's understanding of organic interrelations (1971, p.26), and other critics have noted that the plot of a Dickens novel is very much like such a city: everything is interrelated, but the connections are concealed and very highly mediated. James M. Brown notes that in his mature work Dickens arrives at 'a critical understanding of industrial society through his observation of the city population and the city landscape', and that London descriptions in his novels function artistically as 'an index of the moral life of the whole society' (1982, pp.34, 35). This is a far cry from the early view of Dickens as a social reformer concerned with specific abuses.

Narrative and form

'Narrative' is a word that has become very fashionable in recent years so far as criticism of the novel is concerned, but like many other fashionable things it has existed under other names as a topic for discussion for a long while. A novel is *narrated:* that is to say, the information we receive from its pages comes to us from a *particular* point of view or ostensible source (or, of course, from a number of such sources). Just as it makes a difference in a film or a television play where the director puts his cameras, what angles they have on the action, how they move, so too the way we read a novel is fundamentally directed by the nature of its narration.

In a famous passage on *Bleak House* in his book *Aspects of the Novel*, the novelist and critic E.M. Forster drew attention to the complex shifts of narrative in the novel. He pointed out that in chapter 1 we have an omniscient (literally, 'all-knowing') viewpoint: the narrator knows everything. In chapter 2, according to Forster, the narrator's eyes begin to grow weak, as although he can explain Sir Leicester Dedlock to us he can only explain part of Lady Dedlock, and nothing of Mr Tulkinghorn. And in chapter 3 the narrator (Forster actually refers to Dickens rather than to a narrator) 'goes straight across into the dramatic method and inhabits a young lady, Esther Summerson'. He further adds the shrewd point that, even when Esther is ostensibly narrating, Dickens may snatch the pen from her and take notes himself, implying by this that Dickens's own personality sometimes breaks through that which he has established for Esther (1927, p.86).

According to Forster the reader tolerates these shifts in narrative because Dickens 'bounces' us, but he also remarks rather tartly that 'critics are more apt to object than readers' (p.87). Critics certainly have had a lot to say about the narrative of *Bleak House*, and particularly with regard to Esther Summerson. Esther is not just a narrator in the novel: she is also a rather central character, and for this reason it is very hard to discuss 'narrative' in *Bleak House* without also discussing characterisation. It is fair to say that Esther is the major 'problem' of *Bleak House*, inasmuch as it is around her character and narrative that most critical debate on the novel has taken place.

The double narrative

So far as the double narrative is concerned, we can say that critics divide according to whether they see the two viewpoints as complementary or contradictory, and according to whether they agree with Forster that the 'bouncing' works – or not. Peter K. Garrett relates the technique to a general desire on Dickens's part in his later novels to present both the truth of individual experience and also a comprehensive vision of the world that transcends the limits of individual points of view (1980, p.30). Garrett talks of the 'necessity and incongruity' of these two perspectives, which suggests that Dickens is not to be condemned if there are tensions between the two, and indeed Garrett adds that in *Bleak House,* in spite of the (anonymous) narrator's attempts to involve the reader, 'the disparity persists' [ibid.] Leonard W. Deen – who, like E.M. Forster, points out that the anonymous narrator is not (as some have referred to him) 'omniscient', as there are some things he does not know – argues that at their most extreme divergence the two narrative points of view are perhaps simply incompatible. Deen describes them as 'the sentimental and the ironic-satiric', and suggests that they seem almost a product of schizophrenia (1961, p.55). This relates the double narrative to alleged divisions in Dickens the man, as do Richard Barickman, Susan MacDonald and Myra Stark in their book *Corrupt Relations,* in which they suggest that the extremes of satire and sentiment originate in ambivalence, and are hermetically isolated from each other in the divided narrative structure of *Bleak House.* They point to the important fact that there is no communication between the two narrators 'or the contradic-tory urges they embody' (1982, p.45).

H.M. Daleski draws attention to the separate 'worlds' of the two narrators, with the anonymous narrator dealing with the world of fashion, the world of squalor, and Lady Dedlock, who mediates between the two; while Esther is on the whole concerned with the Bleak House world of middle-class respectability, and it is within her narrative that Chancery is mostly scrutinised (1970, p.157). It is worth noting in passing that this division of narratives may well take us back to the 'anatomy of society', suggesting as it does a separation from each other of nonetheless interdependent aspects of Dickens's society.

Dennis Walder also relates the two narrative positions to Dickens himself, suggesting that the tension between the faith of Esther Summerson and the 'corrosive despair' of the anonymous narrator reflects the ambivalence of Dickens's own final position (1981, p.145). This is very close to Janet L. Larson's suggestion that Esther's religious mythos (i.e. the supernatural pattern of meaning in her narrative) generally counters the fury and despair of the other narrator's chaos

(1983, p.136).

If some of these comments have suggested that there are problems, unresolved tensions, contradictions in the dual narrative of *Bleak House*, a number of critics have no doubt that the technique is an intrinsic part of the novel's greatness. Harvey Peter Sucksmith argues that the alternation between the two viewpoints helps to focus both the 'sympathetic' vision and also the 'ironic' one (1970, p.131n.); M.D. Zabel stresses that it is by the alternation of the two narratives that Dickens achieves something new in his art, 'a depth of focus, a third dimension in his perspective, a moral resonance, and an implicit ambiguity of sympathy and insight' (1956, p.337).

Critics have not generally had much to disagree about so far as the anonymous narrator and his narrative are concerned, so I shall restrict my discussion of this aspect of *Bleak House*.

Esther's narrative

From the earliest responses to the novel we encounter debate around – or reaction against – the character and narrative of Esther. The early reviews are again a useful point of reference: 'the over-perfect Esther', who is 'too precociously good, too perpetually self-present, and too helpful to every one around her to carry a sense of reality' – thus speaks the *Athenaeum* (Dyson, 1969 a, pp. 53, 54). The same review adds a very significant observation: 'nor are her virtues made more probable by the fact that she is the chronicler of her own perfection – though with disclaimers manifold' (p.54). This latter point is focused sharply in a comment in a review in the *Spectator:* 'Such a girl would not write her own memoirs, and certainly would not bore one with her goodness till a wicked wish arises that she would either do something very "spicy", or confine herself to superintending the jam-pots at Bleak House' (Dyson, 1969 a, p.57).

The fact that Esther *writes* her narrative is, I suspect, crucial. In this context there is a very interesting review of a war-time radio dramatisation of *Bleak House*, in which the reviewer, Gwen Major, comments that

'The words Angela Baddeley [who played Esther] used were Esther's, but with her art how charming, how fresh, how spontaneous and altogether

artless they sounded! Gone entirely was the pedantry or smugness the
written word had conveyed to many of us. For the first time I really loved
Esther!'   (1944, p.66).

In my final section I shall be discussing the implications of this
observation and asking whether it is the *written* form of Esther's
narrative (the anonymous narrative is not identified as either
spoken, 'thought' or written) that has caused Dickens
problems.

Talking about Esther, the critic can concentrate on her role
as character, her role as narrator, or both. Clearly it is possible
to argue that Esther is a good narrator but a 'bad' character – or
vice-versa. Esther has had her defenders on both counts, as I
shall show, but very many readers and critics have had their
doubts about one or both of these aspects of her rôle in the
novel.

Robert Garis, in what is perhaps a deliberately provocative
piece of exaggeration, claims that no one has ever thought
Esther a success as a realised character, and that she has been
both quietly detested and actively ignored. He goes further,
arguing that what bothers us is that 'she is empty', that 'she has
no convincing inner life', and that 'she has no will, no sense of
ego, hardly an identity at all' (1965, pp.141, 142). For Garis
'Esther Summerson' (his quotation marks!) is merely an
extremely thin verbal mask over the powerful voice of Dickens
himself (p.108). For John Carey Esther's smallpox means
nothing to us because so far as we are concerned 'she has no
face' (1973, p.61). This anatomical deficiency is, for Angus
Wilson, more extensive: for him her smallpox is a problem
because 'she has no body upon which a head could rest' (1962,
p.438). James H. Broderick and John E. Grant limit their
complaint to the objection that Esther's words 'fail . . . to give
her an effective personality: she is "cloying", "insipid", "too
good to be true-to-life"' (1958, p.252).

George Bernard Shaw found Esther a 'maddening prig',
although he added the reluctant admission that such paragons
do exist (1937, p.284).

Edgar Johnson, in the chapter of his biography of Dickens
which is reprinted in the *Bleak House Casebook*, admits that
Esther is completely successful neither as a character nor as an
instrument of the story's literary technique, but he adds the
telling comment that the fact that she exasperates us 'reveals

that she has genuinely been endowed with life' (Dyson 1969 a,
pp. 139, 140). This can serve as a response to Robert Garis's
claim that Esther has often been quietly detested: how do we
detest someone who does not exist?

Esther has, of course, had her defenders. Some have
restricted themselves to a defence of her rôle as narrator. Thus
W.J. Harvey suggests that if Dickens fails to create a lively
Esther it is because he deliberately suppresses his natural
exuberance in order to create a 'flat Esther' who becomes a
brake which controls the runaway tendency of Dickens's
imagination (1965, p.226).

If this sounds a bit like damning with faint praise, there have
been those ready with less-faint praise. Two important essays
have offered interestingly different defences of Esther as
character and as narrator. Q.D. Leavis, in her study of the
novel, refers to Esther as 'the truly sensitive recording
consciousness of the book', and she insists very forcibly on the
need to explain her apparent self-praise by reference to her
illegitimacy. Mrs Leavis suggests that Esther has so much
difficulty believing people when they praise her that she writes
their praise down so that she *can* believe it (1970, pp.150, 156).

A.E. Dyson has also provided a sustained and challenging
defence of Esther both as narrator and as character. For Dyson,
Esther is a skilled narrator who is able to create complex
'Dickensian' characters for us. As a character she is highly
observant, intelligent in a moral and intuitive way,
self-knowing and capable of self-sacrifice, and entirely without
malice (1969 b, p.262). Dyson attempts to explain Esther's
unpopularity historically: her virtues of patient suffering and
domestic affection 'seem curiously alien to our present time'
(p.265).

If there have been very conflicting views of Esther, there have
also been very strikingly divergent views concerning the last
topic I want to deal with in this section: the plot of *Bleak House*.

Plot

I suspect that one of the things that many modern readers will
be most surprised by is how very dismissive early reviewers
were of Dickens's plot. The *Spectator* review found in it not

simply faults, 'but absolute want of construction'; the *Illustrated London News* regretted that, 'most unfortunately, Mr Dickens fails in the construction of a plot'; *Bentley's Miscellany* found fault with the number of characters who had no influence upon the action of the novel and did not contribute to its catastrophe (climax), adding that 'the story has not been carefully constructed'; *Putnam's Magazine* suggested that Dickens was content to satisfy his readers with single characters 'and has not attempted to add to their value by weaving them together in a plot'; while, finally, the *Eclectic Review* concluded sadly that it 'is doubtful, whether, in any circumstances, [Dickens] could work out a good plot' (Dyson, 1969 a, pp. 56, 60, 71, 73, 75, 81).

Now, to set such comments in context one should perhaps point out that *Bentley's Miscellany* signalled its sensitivity to *Bleak House* by deploring 'the almost entire absence of humour': clearly reviewers can say silly things through ignorance and incompetence. But such a negative consensus should cause us to wonder. Can it be that all these reviewers understood 'plot' rather differently from, say, T.S. Eliot, who thought *Bleak House* 'Dickens's finest piece of construction' (1967, p.279)? Or – if a less highbrow witness is required – Agatha Christie, who as Andrew Sanders reports, exclaimed after attempting to write a film script of the novel, 'such a good plot . . .!' (1982, p.141). T.A. Jackson finds *Bleak House* the most carefully constructed of all Dickens's novels (1937, p.97), a view which echoes John Forster's opinion that 'in the very important particular of construction' the novel is 'perhaps the best thing done by Dickens' (1872–4, II, p.114).

For Edmund Wilson *Bleak House* required of Dickens 'a new use of plot' which made possible a tighter construction. Wilson argues that Dickens responded successfully to this challenge by 'creating the detective story which is also the social fable' (1941, p.32).

For Edgar Johnson, in contrast to the early reviewers, the danger is not lack of plot but a threat that Dickens's 'intricate structures' may seem contrived and overmelodramatic. Johnson feels, however, that in fact we get in *Bleak House* 'a strength in tightness and intensity of development' along with a sense of 'taut inevitability' (Dyson, 1969 a, p.138).

One of the few recent critics of *Bleak House* who tempers praise of the novel with reservations about the plot comparable to those of the early reviewers is Norman Friedman. He finds it sufficiently clear on its own terms, but 'somewhat sprawling and overlarge', as well as being possessed of an apparently thin and sentimental organising-principle (1975, p.360). He does, however, suggest that this seeming paradox of an 'overdevelopment of texture and underdevelopment of structure' may be resolved by an analysis of symbolism which will demonstrate links between these two elements.

Women, Sexuality and the Family: Feminist Responses to 'Bleak House'

As could be expected from its large measure of overt comment upon the role of women in society, *Bleak House* has been of particular interest to critics writing during the last decade and a half, when feminist ideas have had such an extensive influence in literary criticism. Many recent critics who are neither women nor feminist have clearly been influenced by feminist ideas in their response to the novel, even if this has been manifest only in a sharpened interest in such matters as the role and nature of women, 'femininity' and sexuality, and the family. But *Bleak House* triggered off what we may quite legitimately call 'feminist' responses right from its first publication, even if the best-known of these came from a man. John Stuart Mill, writing to his wife in March 1854, was indignant:

> That creature Dickens, whose last story *Bleak House,* I found accidentally at the London Library the other day and took home and read, much the worst of his things, and the only one of them I altogether dislike, has the vulgar impudence in this thing to ridicule rights of women. It is done too in the very vulgarest way, just the style in which vulgar men used to ridicule 'learned ladies' as neglecting their children and household.   (1854, p.95)

Mill's objection is in some ways comparable to the 'social reformer' criticisms of *Bleak House* about which I wrote in my first section; it is clearly concerned with direct references to 'issues' in the novel. We can imagine that Mill particularly objected to the portrayal of Mrs Jellyby, who, in addition to her other charitable interests, has by chapter 67 of the novel, taken up the rights of women to sit in Parliament. There is also Miss

Wisk, who in chapter 30 of the novel talks much of 'woman's mission'.

Subsequent feminist critiques of *Bleak House,* while not ignoring these direct references to the role and position of women, have paid more and more attention to what we can refer to as more implicit comments on attitudes regarding women.

Dickens's view and treatment of women is a massive topic, covering not just the books he wrote but also his private and public relations with women. George Orwell dismissed scornfully the attempt to relate Dickens's fictional treatment of women to his allegedly regrettable treatment of his own wife, saying that this was on the level of relating *Hamlet* to the notorious fact that Shakespeare left his wife his second-best bed in his will (1940, p.414). The parallel seems less powerful in the light of many present-day feminist attempts to relate public and private aspects of a writer's life to an all-embracing *ideology* or set of consistent attitudes, and many recent commentaries on *Bleak House* have freely moved from textual criticism to consideration of Dickens's relationship with his wife (from whom he insisted on parting after she had borne ten of his children, in 1858). We can avoid a concern with too much of the more salacious speculation concerning Dickens's alleged sexual relationship with the young actress Ellen Ternan, as it refers to a time subsequent to the writing of the novel we are looking at. But Dennis Walder's point, that some of the treatment of campaigning women in *Bleak House* may be attibuted to Dickens's having felt personally threatened by such activities, as at that time his wife was involved in an anti-slavery campaign and helping to produce a petition from British to American women on this topic, cannot be discounted (1981, p.164).

The women of 'Bleak House'

To talk about the portrayal of women in *Bleak House* is to move into an area in which it is hard merely to 'stick to the words on the page'. When Walter Savage Landor – who served at least in part as the model for Boythorn – claimed that Dickens had shown that he was with Shakespeare the greatest of English

writers, 'though indeed his women are superior to
Shakespeare's' (quoted by George H. Ford, 1955, p.56), we
have to assess Landor's view of women as much as Dickens's
depiction of them. And, when we contrast such a statement
with George Gissing's comment that Dickens was incapable of
representing any woman save 'the eccentric, the imbecile, and
the shrew (there are at most one or two small exceptions)'
(Dyson, 1969 a, p.94), then we realise – I think – that critical
comments on Dickens's women often tell us as much about the
critics as they tell us about Dickens's novels. Gissing also made
the very interesting suggestion that all of Dickens's novels were
written for masculine readers, and that now (i.e. the turn of the
century) very few women open a volume of his works 'by
deliberate choice' (quoted in Ford, 1955, p.8).

I want, now, to detail three relatively separate areas of
concern in *Bleak House* for feminist critics: the Victorian family
and home; the novel's treatment of sexuality; and critical
accounts which attempt to further understanding of Dickens's
work by noting that he often works in terms of recognisable and
recurrent character *types,* even stereotypes. This last will, I
hope, lead into my subsequent consideration of the critical
response to the characterisation of the novel.

'*Bleak House*' and the family

In a recent book on Dickens, P.J.M. Scott makes the interesting
point that the Chancery disputes which we are shown in *Bleak
House* 'have all originated in *family quarrels* – the Jarndyces',
Miss Flite's, Gridley's' (1979, p.109). This is one of the many
fascinating interconnections in the novel, interconnections
which justify our referring to *Bleak House* as an *organic* structure
– in other words a structure in which all of the parts are related,
directly or indirectly, to one another. Richard Barickman and
his fellow authors of the book *Corrupt Relations* also note that, the
more Esther tells us how thoroughly blessed she is with her
husband, house and children, 'the more aware we are likely to
be of how unresolved the novel has left the social disorder of
England's other families – from the Court of Chancery, which
thrives on family disputes, to the abandoned children of
London's slums' (1982, p.18). T.A. Jackson points out that

Esther is one of a total of three, possibly four, heroes and heroines of Dickens who are children of a 'free-marriage' union, and he argues that Dickens's handling of all of these cases makes it clear that his attitude to 'the bourgeois family' was 'a radically critical one' (1937, p.278). He further argues that the 'charming study' of the Bagnet household, in which of course the 'presiding genius' is a *woman* not a man, gives us further grounds for seeing Dickens's attitude to 'bourgeois households' as thoroughly negative (pp. 284, 285).

Jackson's Marxism may be too extreme for many, but critics of rather different persuasions have had similar things to say. Leonard W. Deen argues that the burden of Esther's story 'is the perversion or crippling of the family and the child' (1961, p.46), and Richard Barickman *et al* state baldly that in Dickens's fiction the typical family 'is inadequate at best, vicious at worst; and the figure who absolutely haunts his fiction is the abandoned, orphaned, or abused child' (1982, p.62). This, it should be noted, easily takes us back to Dickens's biography: his feeling of having been abandoned by his parents as a child (about which one can read in any of the biographical accounts of Dickens available). This is not, of course, to claim an exclusively biographical meaning here: Dickens was not the only Victorian child whose parents neglected him.

Sexuality

Clearly we are not here concerned with overt portrayal of the directly sexual. But John Carey has argued that Dickens's portrayal of both Esther Summerson and the hero of *David Copperfield* demonstrates that he was aware of his own sexual inhibitions, as both 'amount to extended studies of the deviations which Victorian attitudes to sex could promote' (1973, p.169). He argues that her childhood guardians make sexuality terrifying to Esther, that her godmother has a stroke and dies just as Esther is about to read the biblical passage about the woman taken in adultery, that Esther then goes and buries her doll, 'thus renouncing motherhood', that as with David Copperfield 'a homosexual phase follows', and that, although she is revolted when she chances upon a hideous boy fondling and sucking the spikes in Chancery Lane, she can tolerate feminine men such as Prince Turveydrop and paternal men such as Jarndyce, who, Carey suggests, subdues his sexual impulses by open windows and cold baths (1973, p.172).

All this may leave the reader breathless (or infuriated), and it has to be said that Carey mixes a number of shrewd points and wild assertions together here. However, other critics have had not dissimilar things to say about Esther. W.J. Harvey, for example, notes that it is curious that the emotions aroused by the Esther–Ada relationship seem more intense – and more intensely rendered – than those aroused by Esther's encounter with Lady Dedlock (1965, p.229). They are also more intense, I would suggest, than those apparently aroused by Esther's relationship with Woodcourt – although here we have to accept that she may reasonably be thought to be concealing her feelings.

Carey argues that the features that make Esther unwholesome to the modern reader, such as her middle-aged postures, her self-disparagement, and her eagerness for 'unsexing' nicknames, are all shrewdly observed symptoms of a young girl's painful inhibitions about sex – a point that can be set alongside the opinions I quoted previously from Mrs Leavis concerning the effect of her illegitimacy on Esther.

Richard Barickman et al make the interesting suggestion that the whole point of the marriage proposal from Jarndyce, and of Esther's response to it, is to show how satisfying such a marriage would be to the personality Esther professes, and how unsatisfying to needs that she conceals more from herself than from the reader (1982, p.81). James H. Broderick and John E. Grant add the important point that by not marrying Jarndyce Esther avoids her mother's mistake of marrying the wrong man – old and rich (1958, p.257). John Carey sees Dickens's portrayal of Esther as one which combats tendencies in Dickens himself, in particular the tendency to admire plucky, sexless heroines who have an unnatural attachment to older men. Carey cites Little Nell and Little Dorrit as examples (1973, p.173), and there is little doubt that Esther represents an advance upon both of these.

Michael Slater argues that the odd gift of Esther to Woodcourt by Jarndyce at the end of *Bleak House* is an example of Dickens's personal preoccupations 'warping his art into some peculiar shapes' (1983, p.167). He notes that the whole affair 'seems very odd and strained and readers who are made uncomfortable by it are surely right in such a response'. Some sort of identification of himself with Jarndyce certainly, and perhaps also with Woodcourt, may be indicated by the episode; Slater suggests that Dickens's concern for his unmarried sister-in-law Georgina Hogarth was an important element in his attitude towards Esther's marriage prospects, with the older man (Jarndyce) significantly helping her to a suitable husband.

Dickensian stereotypes

The topic of character types or stereotypes in Dickens's work in general and *Bleak House* in particular cannot be separated from Dickens's treatment of the family and of sexuality. Richard Barickman *et al* list a number of these recurrent types: the benevolent but troubled patriarch, the innocent, gentle but addled young man, the unmarried woman who seethes with hostility and bristles with masculine mannerisms, and the angelic young woman who mothers her father or a fatherly old man (often not so much a young woman as a female child) (1982, pp.97, 98). And, as we have already noted, there is the omnipresent neglected child.

Looking at these examples one by one, it is not too difficult to find examples of them in *Bleak House*. G.K. Chesterton has referred to Dickens's peculiar affection for a strange sort of little girl, one with a premature sense of responsibility and duty (1906, p.95), and both Charley and Esther, and, to a certain extent, Caddy, conform to this description in *Bleak House*. Alexander Welsh talks of Dickens's fondness for portraying his heroines as both woman and child (1973, p.154), and Richard Barickman *et al*, suggest that the heroines function as sexually neutral figures who have to struggle even to acknowledge their own personal sexual identity (1982, p.75). Interestingly, they also argue that the intervention of the plot is required to accomplish these romantic resolutions, which the heroines themselves lack the self-confidence or self-awareness to pursue. The application of this description to Esther's case is not too difficult.

Of bad parents we have no shortage in the novel: Mrs Jellyby, Mr Turveydrop, the Smallweed clan, Mrs Snagsby (in

her relation to Guster), Mr Chadband (in his relation to Jo),
Mr Skimpole, Esther's godmother, and even (unwittingly it is
true) Lady Dedlock. And as the Court of Chancery is placed *in
loco parentis* (in the place of parents) over Ada and Richard, it,
too, may be seen to be one of the 'parents' of *Bleak House* who are
found wanting.

So far as the benevolent patriarchs are concerned, we have, of
course, Jarndyce, a man who, like many similar characters in
Dickens, could well have been modelled on one of the
benevolent figures of Oliver Goldsmith (?1730–74) – one of
Dickens's favourite authors. John Carey writes of Dickens's
need to combine the roles of lover and father, referring to the
novelist's extraordinary attachment to his wife's sister Mary
Hogarth, who died at the age of eighteen. Carey remarks
sarcastically that wives who regress so drastically as to
resemble babies or toys 'are accounted particularly palatable',
and he claims that Dickens seemed to have been incapable of
imagining any process whereby a young girl grew into a
middle-aged woman (1973, pp.159, 160). George Orwell refers
to that 'recurrent Dickens figure, the Good Rich Man', who is
needed to solve all the problems to which Dickens had no other
solution (1940, p.417).

Of sexless, or feminine, men we have the examples of Prince
Turveydrop and Mr Snagsby, while the passionate, unmarried
woman is to be found in Mlle Hortense. Lady Dedlock, though
married, is clearly also a version of Dickens's type of the
'passionate woman'. John Carey claims that what Dickens was
unable to do was to show how the sort of passion that his
'passionate women' possess could combine with purity and a
concern with humdrum household duties in a single individual
(1975, p.166). We need to consider whether or not this is true,
or whether Dickens succeeds in doing just this in his portrayal
of Esther.

Finally, we have the abandoned child: in different ways Jo,
Charley, Esther – and Richard and Ada – are abandoned
children. But Mrs Jellyby also abandons her offspring, as, in a
sense, does Mr Turveydrop. Many critics have related such
recurrent figures to Dickens's own upbringing, and we must
also examine, later, the suggestion that one of the major themes
of *Bleak House* is that of the abandonment of parental
responsibilities.

Doubles and 'split-selves'

There is one, concluding, issue that needs to be dealt with in this section. Dickens's work, as many critics have pointed out, is riddled with 'split-selves' and 'doubles'. Jacob Korg asserts that, through a process of doubling, nearly every character in the novel becomes a member of a pair or a series that varies or contrasts one essential characteristic. Thus he points out that Esther is paralleled by Charley, that Lady Dedlock disguises herself as Hortense and later exchanges clothes with Jenny, and that there are two wills, two Bleak Houses, and three husbands for Mrs Bayham Badger (1968, p.2). James M. Brown lists a number of 'split–men' in Dickens's novels, including Inspector Bucket from *Bleak House,* and suggests that this is related to the separation of the private person from the public person in Victorian England (back to the anatomy of society!) (1982, p.23). Mrs Leavis, incidentally, makes a similar point about Inspector Bucket (1970, p.139); I shall have more to say about the Inspector in my final section. J. Hillis Miller notes how many characters in the novel lose a sense of their own existence; at different parts of the novel both Skimpole and George speak of themselves as if they were a third person, (1958, pp. 175, 176), and even Esther has a moment of thinking that she is not really the person she seems to be. (Recall the earlier argument about the self that she admits to herself and the self that she disguises from herself.) The reason why this discussion is in the present section, however, is that many critics have suggested that Dickens reconciled conflicting attitudes in himself and in his audience by as it were 'parcelling them out' to different characters or parts of characters. (For a similar point see Susan R. Horton [1981, p.7].) And among these contradictory attitudes were many concerned with women, sexuality and the family.

In short, such splittings and doublings can lead in many different ways: to the divisions and contradictions in Dickens himself, to divisions and contradictions in his society in general, and to specific divisions and contradictions in attitudes towards such things as sexuality and the family, and towards women. Does the 'doubling' of Hortense and Lady Dedlock suggest that Dickens saw passion as destructive, even murderous? What about Caddy marrying a man as weak as her father – does this give us some clue concerning Dickens's view of gender roles and their reproduction? And what about the fact that the Lord Chancellor, in charge of the institution most vehemently attacked in the work, seems to be a rather pleasant figure in personal terms (thus resembling the unfortunate 'Coavinses' – Charley's father – who has an unpleasant profession but is a model father)?

Perhaps the most interesting study of *Bleak House* from an overtly feminist point of view is Ellen Moers's. Moers accepts that the novel shows that Dickens's immediate, surface reaction to mid-century feminism was one of 'clear hostility' (1973, p.13), but she suggests that the women of *Bleak House* look different, as a group, from the other women of Dickens: 'more forceful, more independent, more capable' (ibid.). She argues that the fact that the novel is full of 'strong women' is, in part, 'what subtly but pervasively alters the love relationships, tilts the emotional centre, and shifts the masculine point of view in the novel (p.16). She further points out that there is much talk of divorce in the novel, that unusually for Dickens it contains a woman who is strong enough to pursue a man (even if, in Lady Dedlock's case, it is only to the grave) (pp. 18, 19), and that the strength of the women in the novel is in sharp contrast to what is the familiar world of *Bleak House* – a world of weakness and confusion, futility and paralysis (p.20).

Moers presents *Bleak House* as a novel divided against itself: hostile to mid-century feminism on the surface, but positively responsive to the changing role of women in society at a deeper level. We have much to consider when one critic finds Esther 'strong', while for others she has no head, no body and no existence. Is it an accident that women critics have, generally, a more positive view of Esther?

Character

There are two words which, quite properly, seem to be inescapable in any discussion of Dickens or his work. They are 'character' and 'humour'. About the second of these I have, perhaps unfortunately, had little so far to say – an omission that will be rectified in my final section. So far as character is concerned, it will be seen that it has been more or less impossible to talk about *Bleak House* without referring to Dickens's characters, however much some modern critics may feel that 'character' is a misleading or outmoded concept.

But it is not just modern critics who have had misgivings about Dickens's characters. While the 'common reader' has repeatedly expressed admiring wonderment at Dickens's ability to create characters, and the term 'a Dickensian character' has entered into the English language, critics have often had reservations concerning this aspect of Dickens's art. There are certain of these reservations that recur very regularly: Dickens's characters have no inner life; they are caricatures rather than characters; they are non-interacting, so locked up in their own identity that they can relate to none other. The contemporary *Spectator* review from which I have already quoted gives a representative early opinion: 'The love of strong effect, and the habit of seizing peculiarities and presenting them instead of characters, pervade Mr Dickens's gravest and most amiable portraits, as well as those expressly intended to be ridiculous and grotesque' (Dyson, 1969 a, p.57).

We should remember that this comment occurs in the specific context of a review of *Bleak House,* and it seems that this work raises the 'problem' of Dickens's characterisation in an especially sharp manner. But many critics have been content to generalise about the shortcomings of Dickens's characters. George Orwell suggests that Dickens's characters are always finished and perfect, they are 'always in a single unchangeable attitude, like pictures or pieces of furniture', and thus the reader cannot hold an imaginary conversation with one of them (1940, p.456).

Inner life

Robert Garis refers to 'the commonplace' that Dickens's characterisation is rendered from an external perspective, and explains this in terms of his theory of Dickens as 'theatrical artist': 'the disinterested, morally intelligent search for the centre of self of human beings' is 'totally at variance with the procedures and attitudes of theatrical art' (1965, pp. 53, 54). Garis sees Dickens's attempts to render the inner life as 'demonstrations by exception of the rule that we do not ordinarily think of him as someone who very often wondered what it was like to be another person' (p.60).

This sort of criticism has been aimed with particular force at *Bleak House*, with Lady Dedlock and Mr Tulkinghorn very often singled out as two characters who have no inner life. However, there is ample evidence that Dickens believed the truth to be that his characters were rendered from the inside. John Forster quotes from a letter of his written during the composition of *David Copperfield* in which Dickens complained of a novel written by an unnamed fellow writer that 'It seems to me as if it were written by somebody who lived next door to the people, rather than inside of 'em' (1872–4, II, p. 58).

And some critics of *Bleak House* have seen the depiction of seemingly 'flat' or 'empty' characters such as Lady Dedlock and Tulkinghorn as something radically different from a mere failure to portray inner lives. P.J.M. Scott, for example, argues that if Dickens had not created Lady Dedlock's 'immaterial' inner life then he would not have created a work as profound as he has (1979, p.63). Grahame Smith suggests that it is crucial to the meaning of *Bleak House* that 'certain levels of human personality should be deliberately enigmatic' (1974, p.34). We can also recall T.A. Jackson's assertion that the fact that Dickens drew caricatures rather than characters should be accounted a virtue, as, by so doing, he saw men as the caricatures of themselves that they were in daily life – that they were made by their circumstances (1937, p.253). And Susan Horton suggests very interestingly that the 'gaps' in the narrator's knowledge of certain characters in *Bleak House* put a particularly fruitful pressure on the reader of *Bleak House*. To this suggestion I shall return in Part Two.

Two critics have argued very strongly that Dickens was antagonistic to his characters: jealous of them or unsympathetic to their need for independence. Robert Garis sees Dickens as a 'social lion' who did not want any of his characters to be rivals (1965, p.65); Mark Lambert notes how often the Dickensian narrator interrupts characters, and sees in this a sort of aggression (just as it is when we interrupt someone in real life). The aggression, for Lambert, springs from Dickens's being hostile towards his characters because he envies the attractiveness they have for the novels' readers (1981, pp. 48, 35).

Character and profession

Before I move on to considering particular characters in *Bleak House* I want to touch on another common critical observation about Dickens's characters – that they are very often portrayed as products, or extensions, of the profession or trade they follow. Of Tulkinghorn, the contemporary *Spectator* reviewer remarked that he

> is a capital instance of an old trick of Mr Dickens, by which the supposed tendencies and influences of a trade or profession are made incarnate in a man, and not only is "the dyer's hand subdued to what it works in", but the dyer is altogether eliminated, and his powers of motion, his shape, speech, and bodily functions, are translated into the dye-tub.   (Dyson, 1969 a, p.58)

This is a difficult quotation, but put simply it argues that characters in Dickens are not just affected by their work: their personalities become so subdued to this work that they disappear altogether, so that what we are left with is a sort of personified job. Tulkinghorn, in this view, is not a man influenced by his job but a sort of 'walking job' which has lost all human characteristics.

Edgar Johnson makes a similar point about *Bleak House*, observing that Dickens's portrayal of characters such as Sir Leicester Dedlock or the Lord Chancellor, or Carboy, Kenge and Inspector Bucket, refuses to make them *personally* responsible for the evil they do. As he says, individually they may all be amiable enough, 'but they are instruments of a system' (Dyson, 1969 a, p.147). (This should be compared with T.A. Jackson's comment on the lack of an individual villain in *Bleak House*.) As J. Hillis Miller puts it, characters such as Krook and the Lord Chancellor are 'sinister only in their representative capacities' (1971, p.16).

When we turn to a consideration of critical views of individual characters in *Bleak House* these more general assertions should be borne in mind; they may well help us to come to terms with some of the critical disagreements we shall meet.

Mr Tulkinghorn

Mr Tulkinghorn is not the most important character in the

novel, but neither is he unimportant. He has provoked some interestingly diverse responses from the critics. A.E. Dyson sees him relatively straightforwardly: he is 'among the two or three most sinister figures that Dickens ever drew' (Dyson, 1969 b, p.248). P.J.M. Scott is more or less in agreement: 'with all the black-rook imagery and the like, he is plainly a bad man' (1979, p.69).

Edgar Johnson is not so far away from such judgements, although he is obviously rather puzzled about Tulkinghorn, referring to the 'almost purposeless malignance' with which he pursues Lady Dedlock – a phrase reminiscent of Coleridge's description of one of Iago's soliloquies: 'the motive-hunting of a motiveless malignity'. Is Tulkinghorn, then, merely evil – and evil in a way that is never explained by Dickens but just taken as a fact? George H. Ford quotes an early comment on *Bleak House* from George Brimley in which Brimley draws attention to the '"purely outward" aspects of character and [Dickens's] failure (with Tulkinghorn for example) to deal with motives' (1955, p.183).

According to most of these critics, then, the portrayal of Tulkinghorn is at best simplistic, at worst a serious artistic flaw on *Bleak House.* Instead of a living character whose actions are explainable by reference to – let us say – personality and situation, we are given a purely evil individual who either has no inner life, or has one which the reader cannot decipher. Tulkinghorn's 'evil' is not related to anything else in *Bleak House;* it is merely something Dickens asserts and expects the reader to accept unquestioningly.

Other critics have seen the matter as more complex than this. Susan R. Horton points out that in describing Mr Tulkinghorn the narrator is as reserved and as cautious as Mr Tulkinghorn himself. She relates this to the narrator's similar lack of omniscience with regard to Miss Flite (see the third page of the novel: 'Some say she really is, or was, a party to a suit; but no one knows for certain, because no one cares'). Horton suggests that the power of many passages of the novel resides in the narrator's refusal to tell the whole truth, and his admission that he does not know the whole truth (1981, pp. 46, 47). As I have suggested, this argument is at least partly based on the theory that the less the narrator tells us the more active the reader has to be, especially in terms of his or her moral intelligence.

Literature which tells the reader everything – so this sort of argument runs – makes the reader passive and uncreative; a novel which forces us to *think* about *why* Tulkinghorn behaves as he does exercises our intellectual capacities. We experience such a novel more as we experience real life (or at least the life of contemporary society), in which we do not have a window onto peoples' inner lives through which to peer.

Still other critics have suggested that Mr Tulkinghorn's inner life may not be obvious, but it can be guessed at by a sensitive and intelligent reader. Mrs Leavis, for example, describes Tulkinghorn as 'an interesting case' who manipulates his employers while despising them, getting his real payment 'by feeding and exercising his desire for power' (1970, p.126). She also notes that Tulkinghorn 'hates women' (p. 135), an interesting suggestion which is worth further consideration. Certainly there is the tantalising passage in the novel which refers to Tulkinghorn's 'double' – 'that one bachelor friend of his' who is a man of the same mould as Tulkinghorn as well as a lawyer, and who, at the age of seventy-five, 'gave his gold watch to his hair-dresser one summer evening, and walked leisurely home to the Temple, and hanged himself' (*Bleak House*, p.359). Are we to assume that Tulkinghorn is homosexual? Certainly the passage concerning his friend reminds us that Dickens does not just work in terms of the isolated individual character: pairs and groups of characters often suggest patterns and explanations which cannot be deduced from individual characters.

Mrs Leavis sees Tulkinghorn as all of a piece and 'thoroughly accounted for', and neither the mystery nor the engine of melodrama that he is commonly considered to be (1970, p.160). She suggests that the only extraordinary thing about him is the contrast between his public self and his private self: while the former is innocuous, the latter it is that really drives him, and he 'lives only in his sense of power, hating Lady Dedlock for having more influence with her husband than himself, and all women for their role in life and that irrational nature of theirs which he can't control' (ibid.).

Note that this interpretation is the reverse of that which sees Tulkinghorn as completely subordinate to his profession: this sees his professional activity as completely subservient to his inner drive for power. Where one critic sees the invasion of the private self by the public self, Mrs Leavis sees the reverse. What is, significantly, not disputed is that it is with regard to the relationship between the public and the private that the clue to Mr Tulkinghorn may lie.

Mr Guppy

Let us turn to another member of the legal profession, Mr Guppy. James M. Brown notes that most of Dickens's lower-class characters express themselves in the specialised vocabulary of their trade or social role, a fact which he sees working against Dickens's insistence that their humanity transcends their specialised function (1982, p.137). Dickens may well have been influenced by another of his favourite authors – Tobias Smollett (1721–71) – here; a character such as Smollett's Commander Trunnion sees the whole world in terms of a vocabulary that his vocation of sailor has given him. G.L. Brook has undertaken a revealing analysis of Mr Guppy's language, which shows that the matter is perhaps a little more complex than Brown suggests. Guppy *does* express himself in legal language in situations where this is inappropriate, and like the letter which Esther receives from Kenge and Carboy (*Bleak House*, p.74) this points to the intrusion of professional – commercial considerations into the humanity of the individual. Brook shows, however, that Guppy's speech (his 'idiolect' in Brook's terminology) is characterised by 'a mixture of levels that arises from the speaker's pre-occupation with class distinctions joined with uncertainty about the kind of language that is appropriate to a particular occasion' (1970, p.165). Analysing the speech Guppy gives when proposing to Esther (*Bleak House*, pp. 174, 175), Brook notes that this shows a mixture of the genteel, the literary (parts are described as 'straight out of the circulating library novels'), and the colloquial (1970, p.165).

George Gissing finds Mr Guppy to be 'chicane incarnate' (Dyson, 1969 a, p.97), while another perceptive early critic of Dickens, his biographer John Forster, lumps 'the Guppys' together with 'Weevles, Snagsbys, Chadbands, Krooks and Smallweeds, even the Kenges, Vholeses, and Tulkinghorns' as 'much too real to be pleasant' (1872–4, II, p.115).

Yet Harvey Peter Sucksmith announces that Guppy 'never ceases to delight us' (1970, p.318), and he explains that the fact that Dickens had himself been a lawyer's clerk ensured that he was able 'to communicate to the reader his own deep-seated sympathy with Guppy' (1970, p.318).

Mrs Leavis, in what is perhaps the most humanely intelligent critical account of the character of Mr Guppy, talks of 'his characteristic mixture of legal jargon and romantic clichés', and notes that Guppy's sentimental idiom and professions never for a moment prevent him from putting his business interests first. Here we may pause to ask whether it is, indeed, his *business* interests that Guppy puts first. But Mrs Leavis continues, very persuasively, to argue that this jargon of Guppy's is remote from anything Guppy really feels. The possibility still remains, however, that the language Guppy uses really does express what he is: especially in its tensions and contradictions.

We may indeed wonder whether the significant thing about the characterisation of Mr Guppy is that it demonstrates his 'decent instincts' – as Mrs Leavis puts it – relegating the heartlessness of the legal jargon to second place. Mr Guppy is not, after all, a particularly successful user of legal chicanery. Mrs Leavis makes a very strong case for us to see Mr Guppy as neither black nor white, but as it were the site of warring contradictions.

And these contradictions are of course very important elsewhere in the novel: we need to remember that 'characterisation' in such a novel as *Bleak House* is not merely a matter of producing more or less lifelike personalities; it is also the means whereby significant themes crucial to the meaning of the novel are further explored.

Skimpole

A good example of this is the character of Skimpole. In a novel so concerned with the issue of parent-child responsibilities, a character who, although adult, insists that he is a child, has more than an individual significance. Much critical discussion of the character of Skimpole (like that of Boythorn) has had a lot to say about the relationship between Skimpole and his

real-life model Leigh Hunt. I don't want to spend time
discussing this issue, but I would like to point out that critics
have seen Skimpole in rather different ways. Skimpole is one of
the many characters in *Bleak House* who are in some sense
divided (see my previous section): as J. Hillis Miller points out,
he talks of himself as if he were a third person (1958, p.176), and
his 'childishness' is clearly intended by Dickens to be a
self-interested camouflage for his unprincipled behaviour.
Dennis Walder talks of Skimpole's 'callousness', but adds that
he exerts an odd, intermittent attraction (1981, p.160); other
critics have found him purely evil. Andrew Sanders points out
that all of the later novels contain characters who are leading
double lives, 'either innocently or culpably' (1982, p.204), and
we have to see Dickens's portrayal of such as Skimpole in the
light of this general tendency to explore alternative human
possibilities through double and split characters.

Robert Garis makes interesting reference to the early
meeting between Skimpole and Coavinses, which he describes
as an encounter between an apparent victim who is really a
parasitic ruler of the System and an official representative of the
System who is really a pathetic victim (1965, p.114). We see
here that 'characterisation' cannot be separated from other
aspects of the novel – in this instance, its concern to anatomise
society through patterned interplay between characters. Peter
K. Garrett points out, for instance, that, although Sir Leicester
Dedlock and Mr Turveydrop have no connection at the level of
plot, they confront each other 'as analogous social fossils and
parasites', and he refers to the description of Dedlock values as
'Dandyism' in the novel (1980, p.44). Skimpole is obviously
another example of such parasitism, and as such his
significance in the novel is not purely personal or individual.

And, if character and theme intermingle, so do character and
environment, as Andrew Sanders points out: with the exception
of Bleak House itself, 'all of the novel's settings share the
dreadful mortality and hopelessness of the burial ground', and
this 'deadness, and the moral and spiritual emptiness, is also
shared by many of the characters'. Sanders relates this
relationship to the 'unity' of *Bleak House,* and notes that the
novel is 'populated by monomaniacs, by the unbalanced, the
repressed, the confused, the proud, the ignorant and the
unbending' (1982, p.150).

Character and social class

Many of Dickens's earliest critics realised that his characters
had a representative quality as well as individual or
idiosyncratic life, and (in a way rather different from that of
more recent critics) they often praised or blamed the novelist's
characterisation in these terms. Dickens was often criticised for
not being able to portray a gentleman, and the contemporary
review in *Bentley's Monthly Review* gives an interesting variant of
this criticism with regard to *Bleak House*. We are told by the
reviewer that Dickens never displays as much power in dealing
with characters from high life as with those in the middle and
lower classes, and exception is taken to Sir Leicester Dedlock
for being, unnaturally, 'simply the incarnation of aristocratic
pride' (Dyson, 1969 a, p.68). George Bernard Shaw responded
vigorously to this sort of criticism. Citing the opinion of a
'leading encyclopaedia' that Dickens had no knowledge of
country gentlemen, Shaw responded vigorously that it would
have been nearer the mark to say that Dickens knew everything
that mattered about Sir Leicester Dedlock and that Trollope
knew nothing that mattered about him. 'Trollope and
Thackeray could see Chesney Wold; but Dickens could see
through it' (1937, p.287).

Inspector Bucket

Inspector Bucket's portrayal in the novel has provoked
considerable discussion concerning Dickens's attitude towards
the police. On the surface, the picture of Inspector Bucket that
we are given seems a positive one, but underneath all sorts of
contradictory tensions (both in the character and in Dickens's
presentation of him) have been detected by critics. So far as
Bucket's bribing of Skimpole, and his 'moving on' of Jo
(moving on to his death, we may recall) are concerned, many
have reluctantly seen the strength of Skimpole's point of view:
'If it is blameable in Skimpole to take the note, it is blameable in
Bucket to offer the note – much more blameable in Bucket,
because he is the knowing man' (*Bleak House*, p.886). Many
critics have commented on Dickens's favourable attitude
towards the police, and have seen his portrayal of Bucket as an

attempt to express this favourable attitude which is partly
sabotaged by Dickens's half-conscious realisation of more
negative elements. John Carey comments that that part of
Dickens's character which enjoyed seeing people ordered and
regimented 'made him a particularly ardent admirer of the
Metropolitan Police Force' (1973, p.39), but Carey (and
others) also points out that there is another, more anarchic part
of Dickens's character which sees such regimentation rather
differently. This, we can presume, perhaps explains the
seeming contradictions in Bucket's character: tactful and
friendly enough to avoid arresting George until an
unembarrassing moment, but ruthless in harrying Jo to his
death.

Mrs Leavis sees Inspector Bucket as a precursor of the
concept of the 'split man' towards which Dickens is, according
to her, feeling his way at this moment. She refers to Bucket's
domestic felicity, fondness for children (when respectable), and
'the strict separation of his everyday good-heartedness from his
bloodhound professionalism' (1970, p.139), a comment that
takes us, fruitfully, in a number of different directions. To begin
with, we can see that we are back to what we have observed
before in *Bleak House:* divisions in characters are related to
divisions in society. The increasing separation of 'home' from
'job', for example, clearly worried many Victorians, and in
Bleak House Dickens dramatises this separation in the character
of Bucket.

Orwell finds it significant that the only officials handled with
any kind of friendliness are policemen (1940, p.429), and we
need to confront a central paradox about *Bleak House:* that it is a
novel in which the law is frontally attacked but in which those
responsible for implementing the law are treated with respect.
Mrs Leavis explains the complexities of Inspector Bucket in
terms of his being in the service of a bad system which he cannot
afford to question or think about (1970, p.138). But does *Bleak
House* lead the reader to think that Bucket serves a bad system,
or is Orwell nearer the mark when he suggests that (on a
conscious level, we may perhaps add) Dickens always admired
the police? M.D. Zabel has drawn attention to the fact that
Bleak House is a 'novel of multiple detectives', with Bucket
supported both by Tulkinghorn and by Guppy (1956, p.339),
and it may well be that Dickens saw parallels between the

mystery-solving function of the detective and the similar function of the novel-reader. If so, his positive attitude towards Bucket (if such there be) may not simply be a matter of his expressing admiration for the police. In *The Old Curiosity Shop* Dickens writes of those who live 'solitarily in great cities as in the bucket of a human well', and this indicates that the Inspector's name maybe suggested something about London to Dickens. Like a well bucket the Inspector also 'descends' into dark and damp places, and Dickens's fascination with him may be the fascination of the unraveller of secrets, the establisher of connections (the latter an important, and consciously emphasised element in *Bleak House*). Janet L. Larson sees Bucket as a sort of godfather who rechristens Esther 'Queen' as they drive through streams of turbulent water in what Larson calls 'a dark baptismal crisis' (1983, p.158). In view of the 'freezing' and 'melting' imagery with which *Bleak House* is packed, we may feel it appropriate, when the thaw comes, that Esther is well provided with a Bucket.

We have come some way from the debate about whether or not Dickens's characters are possessed with an inner life; modern criticism has certainly disagreed about the wider significance that Dickens's characterisation has in *Bleak House*, but that it has that wider significance is no longer in question.

PART TWO: APPRAISAL

Reading 'Bleak House'

IN this part of the book I want to try to get much closer to the actual reading-experience, closer to what the reader undergoes as he or she reads *Bleak House*. A far more explicit concern with the reading-experience has characterised much recent novel criticism; critics have come more and more to realise that something essential is lost if one forgets what it is actually like to be reading a novel. But we must start with a rather important point: there is no single, common 'reading-experience' of a novel such as *Bleak House*. We can ask, 'Which reader?' – does a present-day reader read the novel in the same way as one of Dickens's contemporaries? Then we can ask, 'Which reading?' – for clearly the first time one reads the novel one has a rather different experience of it from on second and subsequent reading-occasions. And we can also ask 'Which experience?' – in other words, at which point of the reading is one making one's investigation: during the reading, or after the novel has been completed?

These may seem rather silly or hair-splitting questions, but they do point us towards certain simple facts which we need to remember when thinking of the critical debate around the novel. First, whatever else he was doing Dickens was attacking contemporary abuses in *Bleak House*, and thus we can expect that for modern readers certain aspects of the novel will have a rather different significance from that they had for readers in the 1850s. Secondly, *Bleak House* is a novel which sets certain *mysteries* before the reader, and we read on to solve these mysteries. Thus our first reading of the novel is always, in a sense, unique: unless we allow many years to elapse before we reread the novel (or we have an extraordinarily bad memory) we can never recapture that desire to know 'what happens' which is one of the impulses that forces us to turn the pages the first time we read the novel, but this may allow us to notice other things on a second reading that our impatience led us to miss the first time. The third point I wish to stress is that an essential part of a reading of such a novel as *Bleak House* – and especially on our first reading of it – consists of the numerous guesses, hypotheses and other imaginings that we engage in as the novel unfolds, even if in strict plot terms these turn out to be blind alleys. Thus after the murder of Tulkinghorn we probably (on a first reading of the novel) consider the possibility that either George or Lady Dedlock may be responsible for his death, and although we eventually discover that neither is actually guilty this suspicion is an important part of the reading-experience; it does not just heighten tension, but also asks us to consider possibilities in the human relationships depicted in the novel which are inherent if unactualised.

Tension is crucial to the reader's experience of *Bleak House*. Not only do we want to learn of the plot's outcome, but our sympathetic involvement with the characters makes us eager to see them rewarded or punished – or at least made aware of the full truth. (Is this perhaps why some readers regret Tulkinghorn's dying without this full knowledge?) Moreover, this element of tension is of increasing importance as we near the end of the novel. It is very easy to neglect this aspect of *Bleak House* in a critical essay: critics have a tendency to write about novels as 'finished objects', or completed experiences, to consider the text as a whole, and to forget the actual reading-experience. But one of the things that has made Dickens such a consistently popular novelist is his ability to write novels that grip the reader. And this is not just a matter of the reader's wanting to know 'what happens', because the experience can be repeated on a subsequent reading. Esther actually becomes far less of a problem for the reader the more she is involved in action, and just as the reader of a detective novel is persuaded to ignore all sorts of inadequacies in the text by the power of curiosity that makes him or her read on excitedly, so too the simple plot tensions and mysteries in *Bleak House* carry the reader along past elements in the work which perhaps do not bear too close a scrutiny. Thus Lady Dedlock's death in the churchyard which contains Hawdon's body is far more than a convenient coincidence: it makes a fitting narrative and thematic climax, linking high and low, past and present, the denial of love and the loss of life. It 'ties up' the plot, but it does much more too.

I should like now to make some more detailed points concerning different readers and readings, and then to comment more personally upon some of the critical debates I have mentioned in the preceding Survey.

According to Mrs Leavis Dickens wrote to be read in two ways, giving what she refers to as 'the Meagles section of his reading-public' (Meagles was a kind but conventional middle-class character in *Little Dorrit*) the moral that it wanted, while allowing the rest of the novel's meaning to sink in less directly (1970, p.121). Dickens had, in his own time, an extremely diverse reading public and there is little doubt that he was aware of this and wrote in such a way as to make contact with these different readers. We should also remember that *Bleak House* appeared first published in instalments, and, although recent critical opinion has absolved Dickens from the charge of having written 'cliffhangers', nevertheless the serial publication must have given early readers a reading-experience different from that enjoyed by a reader who can decide (interruptions apart) how much of the novel he or she will read at one sitting. The end of an instalment will have been significant for an early reader of the novel: if there is no more to read then you inevitably think more about what you have just read, and speculate about what will happen (rather than just reading on, as the reader of *Bleak House* in book form can do).

It is certainly worth paying particular attention to the instalment divisions of the work in any reading of the novel. I want now, however, to spend a few pages making particular reference to the differences between first and subsequent readings of *Bleak House*. We should remember that Dickens is a novelist whose works are very frequently read and reread; if you like Dickens then you are extremely unlikely to stop at just one reading of his novels. But when we reread the novel we do not just *reproduce* our initial reading, as H.M. Daleski points out:

as we read the novel for the first time, the sense of connections being mysteriously made in a way that we cannot quite comprehend is what is principally offered to our bewilderment. (When we reread the novel, our awareness of the mastery with which the connections are prepared for and established is a constant source of pleasure.)   (1970, p.156)

This seems to me to be very well put, and I should like to suggest examples which substantiate Daleski's point.

In chapter 5 – the first chapter of Dickens's second instalment – Esther and Caddy are taken by Miss Flite to Krook's Rag and Bottle Warehouse. Esther describes in some detail the multitude of strange objects and signs visible in the shopwindow, and in the middle of her description we read that

> Some of the inscriptions I have enumerated were written in law-hand, like the papers I had seen in Kenge and Carboy's office, and the letters I had so long received from the firm. Among them was one, in the same writing, having nothing to do with the business of the shop, but announcing that a respectable man aged forty-five wanted engrossing or copying to execute with neatness and dispatch: Address to Nemo, care of Mr Krook within.   (p.99).

Now the alert reader is likely to link this with Lady Dedlock's response to the 'law-hand' in which a legal document brought by Tulkinghorn to her husband is written, about which the reader will have read in chapter 2. But it is only on a second reading of the novel, I strongly suspect, that the idea that Esther is looking at her father's handwriting comes forcibly to the reader. By the time that we learn that Nemo/Captain Hawdon is Esther's father, this scene is far enough back in our memory for us not to feel the need to re-examine it. What we do get, on our initial reading, is a sense of *mystery*, of clues being scattered so profusely that making sense of them seems a hopeless task – at this point.

A few lines further on Krook himself makes his first appearance: 'He was short, cadaverous, and withered; with his head sunk sideways between his shoulders, and the breath issuing in visible smoke from his mouth, as if he were on fire within' (ibid.). A first-time reader, surely, takes this latter detail as one of Dickens's metaphorical flights-of-fancy; on a second reading the knowledge of Krook's forthcoming demise through spontaneous combustion gives this detail an inescapably literal meaning. As Daleski says, the experience is different the second time; knowing the novel relatively well we can enjoy the mastery (as Daleski puts it) with which connections are prepared for and established. But for the first-time reader this detail has the force of metaphorical suggestiveness; it helps to form our conception of Krook's character, without our necessarily being particularly conscious of what is happening.

Many critics fail to make this necessary distinction. Thus P.J.M. Scott is right to say that the reader of *Bleak House* is rendered vulnerable, with those usual privileges of sharing in the author's omniscience and foresight curtailed, but only if he is referring to the first-time reader. Scott compares the experience of reading the novel to 'living itself' (1979, p.78), and this is similar to J. Hillis Miller's suggestion that the situation of many characters in the novel is exactly like that of its writer or reader – interpreting signs or texts (1971, p.11). But again this is most true of our *first* reading of the novel, when we don't know what is to happen, although we are bewildered by mysteries and conscious that many clues can be found in the text. And the mental – and moral – exercise that this situation gives us *does* resemble 'life itself'; reading *Bleak House* for the first time makes us flex our powers of critical discrimination and moral judgement. We read *actively:* puzzling, trying different interpretations, different sets of connections, alternative assessments.

But, if the first-time reading of *Bleak House* is like living, subsequent readings are like thinking back on life. We see things in the novel – connections, parallels, patterns – which we missed on the first reading, just as we do when we think back on life.

Take Skimpole, for instance. My impression is that during our first reading of *Bleak House* our assessment of Skimpole changes consistently and rather painfully. From an enjoyment of the quiddities and quirks of his character we have to move, by uncomfortable reassessment, to a conscious recognition of the evil that such irresponsibility involves. The reader is – in a way reminiscent of Swift – betrayed into admiring that which we are subsequently forced to admit is not at all admirable. On a second reading, in contrast, as we know what to expect we judge Skimpole much more harshly from the beginning, assessing all his values and behaviour in terms of his selfish and cruel denial of other people's humanity.

Moreover, it seems to me that the portrayal of Skimpole works best on a first reading of the novel. When we reread the novel knowing, in a sense, the 'point' Dickens is making, the sections involving Skimpole are rather tedious. We are no longer betrayed, no longer forced so much to examine ourselves through our enjoyment of Skimpole's eccentricities.

But, if this is a loss, we gain a new and perhaps more rewarding perspective on John Jarndyce: we are more critical of his toleration of Skimpole, more sadly aware that his inability to accept and thus to confront human evil is, itself, productive of evil. A second reading of the novel forces the consideration upon us that Jarndyce's kindness to Skimpole and ignoring of his faults leads directly to the death of Jo. Importantly, then, we are made to realise that *Bleak House* does *not* suggest that relatively indiscriminate benevolence is the cure for all ills.

Conscious and unconscious responses

Sooner or later, talking about first and subsequent readings of the novel (or of any novel) we have to mention the vexed issue of 'unconscious' responses – an inadequate term, but I hope that what I mean will become clear shortly. Many students studying a work such as *Bleak House* get somewhat depressed when, after having read and enjoyed the novel they turn to the work of critics and find page after page on patterns of imagery, symbolic meanings, image clusters, and so on. Are they such bad readers as they may be tempted to believe because they have registered none of these things?

Take the images of sun and shadow, ably catalogued and discussed by Norman Friedman (1975). Many first-time readers must finish a careful and enjoyable reading of the novel without having been conscious of this element in the novel. But it is arguable that, even when the reader does not consciously register these intricate patterns of sun–shade reference in the novel, he or she is none-the-less affected by them. Some examples are foregrounded sufficiently for them to be appreciated in themselves – as with the celebrated 'broad bend-sinister of light' cast upon Lady Dedlock's picture in chapter 12 (p.204), and Esther's description of Richard and Ada passing through the light into the shadow at the end of chapter 13 (which is also the end of one of the novel's instalments) (p.233). And if the latter example is overt enough to strike the reader, then the reference to a 'shade' crossing Ada's face on the first page of the next chapter may also set off bells in the reader's mind.

But who, on a first reading of the novel, pays particular attention to the sunny significance of the name of the Sol's Arms? Or links this to the fact that Esther's life is described as having begun with a shadow on it, or that Snagsby's shop is 'shady' and that after his collapse Sir Leicester Dedlock is described as 'a decrepit shadow of himself'? These are all references that on second and subsequent readings are picked up more and more diligently – not least because the reader knows what to look for (perhaps as a result of having read a number of critical accounts of the novel). Someone reading *Bleak House* for the first time may, in other words, be affected by such patterns of imagery without consciously registering their presence. Norman Friedman suggests, interestingly, that such a conscious recognition helps to resolve certain problems concerning the novel for the reader. The same may be true of other image patterns in *Bleak House:* the melting – freezing antithesis, for instance. And think of the numerous references to *birds* in the work: most obviously Miss Flite's unambiguously symbolic creatures, which we are told will be killed by other birds if they are ever released, and which are indeed, ominously, released late on in the novel.

But there is also Boythorn's extraordinary bird, the insistent association of Tulkinghorn with a crow at one point and a rook at another (an important distinction: crows are solitary birds, rooks are not), Skimpole's description of his lodgings as his 'bird's cage' and Inspector Bucket's description of him as 'a queer bird', Volumnia's birdlike hopping about and pecking at papers – all of these combine to make a significant family of references.

If such patterns and repetitions in the novel work on the reader indirectly upon first reading, their conscious recognition upon subsequent readings is likely to move the reader from immersion in the story of *Bleak House* and impatience to follow the plot, in order to discover the secret connections hinted at early on, to a greater awareness of the artistry of the novel – and, along with this, a greater awareness of the patterns of meaning and argument it develops.

The problem of Esther

There are, however, some 'technical' aspects of the novel which force themselves upon the reader from his or her first reading, and the most important of these is the double narrative. I can still remember the disappointment I felt on my first reading of the novel many years ago when I started chapter 3 and realised that the assured, ironic voice of the anonymous narrator was to be abandoned for that of Esther. And Esther *is* a problem in *Bleak House,* not because so many critics have said so but because there are unresolved problems in her narrative which the reading of the novel seems to uncover for most readers.

Part of this rests in technical matters. The anonymous narrator is, in technical parlance, 'extradiegetic': that is to say he (no gender is ever directly attributed to him, but many aspects of the narrative suggest maleness) is not a character in the story as is Esther. His 'telling' is a literary convention; we do not feel impelled to ask how he knows the things he does know, any more than we feel a curiosity concerning the way in which one of Jane Austen's narrators has learned what she tells us. (His use of the present tense certainly makes a significant contribution to the effect of his narrative, making it urbane, detached and familiar). And as I suggested above, the assurance and irony that is a constant element in the anonymous narrator's telling is lacking in Esther's part of *Bleak House.* I do not mean by this that Esther as character is unsure of herself – that is in fact true, but it need not affect the convincingness of her telling. It is more that Dickens seems unsure of Esther's narrative position and function.

This can be seen most clearly in Esther's words at the beginning of chapter 67, where she announces,

> Full seven happy years I have been the mistress of Bleak House. The few words that I have to add to what I have written, are soon penned; then I, and the unknown friend to whom I write, will part for ever. Not without much dear remembrance on my side. Not without some, I hope, on his or hers.   (p.932)

For the first time here, Esther's narrative is given an overtly defined status *within the realistic framework of the story.* But how inadequate it is! Would a character like Esther write as she has done to 'an unknown friend'? Why would she so write? How can she have 'much dear remembrance' for someone she doesn't know?

As I suggested in my earlier section on the double narrative, part of this problem is the fact that Esther is supposedly *writing* her narrative; the commentator who remarked that Esther's words sounded so much more natural spoken in a radio dramatisation of the novel certainly had a point. Think of those repeated occasions, early on, where Esther becomes rather coy about Woodcourt. One such will serve as a fair example: Esther, at the start of chapter 30, is trying to explain why she found Mrs Woodcourt 'irksome', and suggests a number of possible explanations for this, ending with the comment, 'I don't know what it was. Or at least if I do, now, I thought I did not then. Or at least – but it don't matter' (p.467).

This is a classic example of a passage which would work in spoken narrative – but which fails when written. We get confused and say things we can't retract when we're talking, and a writer can use this fact to get characters unwillingly to reveal their secrets. But we don't do this when we're writing, for the simple reason that we are able to cross out words we wish we hadn't written.

Passages such as this show that Dickens had not successfully fixed the technical aspects of Esther's narrative. It may well have been a mistake to make overt the precise nature of her narrative; after all, this is very successfully left undefined in the case of the anonymous narrator (although, of course, he is not a character in the novel). One effect of this – clearly seen in the passage I quote above – is that, where Dickens appears to be trying to show Esther as pleasantly embarrassed, he succeeds in making her appear coy and simpering.

I have quoted a passage from near the end of the novel, but Esther is something of a problem for the reader right from the start of her narrative. As I have said, she becomes less of a problem the more action she is involved in – as when she pursues Lady Dedlock with Inspector Bucket. But a passage such as the following one, which occurs only a few pages after Esther's first entry into the novel, raises rather serious problems for the reader. Esther has just received the letter from Kenge and Carboy which, couched in absurd legal language, talks of her as if she were an inanimate package, to be 'forded, carriage free', to London. Esther comments on the letter effusively, ending as follows: 'but the pleasure of it, and the pain of it, and the pride and joy of it, and the humble regret of it, were so blended, that my heart seemed almost breaking while it was full of rapture' (p.74). This emotional self-indulgence can be treated with equanimity by few readers. Moreover, many readers are unsure whether to see here Dickens snatching Esther's pen and breaking into her narrative, or, rather, to see the words as expressive of Esther's own emotional self-indulgence.

Interestingly, just before the letter from Kenge and Carboy is quoted, Esther starts a paragraph thus: 'Six quiet years (I find I am saying it for the second time) . . .' 'Saying' can be used in a non-literal sense, of course, but passages such as this suggest that Dickens's imagination pictures Esther as talking rather than writing, and that his commitment to her writing her narrative involves serious tensions with his creative instincts. Moreover, the contrast between the Kenge and Carboy letter – behind which Dickens's pointed irony can be seen clearly directed at the manner in which the law dehumanises human relationships – and Esther's total lack of any ironic perspective on herself, again puzzles us. The reader feels baffled: can the writer whose irony bears such eloquent testimony to his ability to see behind people's claims for themselves really take Esther at her own valuation – and expect his reader to do so too? It is doubtless such bafflement that has led to what in my view are some rather far-fetched theories concerning Esther's sexuality. I do not agree with the comment from John Carey, quoted in the Survey, concerning Esther's painful inhibitions about sex; Esther's concealments of her attraction to Woodcourt can be explained more easily in terms of her doubts about his feelings and her social inferiority.

The double narrative

This is a general problem relating to the double narrative: the habits of ironic contemplation that we are encouraged to develop in the sections of *Bleak House* relayed to us by the anonymous narrator are inappropriate to Esther's narrative – indeed, they have a disastrous effect if exercised therein.

This is not to say that the double narrative is all failure: one of the complexities of *Bleak House* is that its successes and failures are inextricably intertwined. The double narrative achieves a number of extremely important effects for the reader. First, it causes him or her continually to 'reset' his or her attitude to what is depicted. We can say that this helps to convey the complexity of the world and of life; we are continually reminded that things look differently from different viewpoints, and so we cannot comfortably relax into 'seeing' the world through one fixed and reliable perspective; as we shift from the anonymous narrator to Esther, and back again, we keep being faced with problems of reconciling their viewpoints and values, and this makes the reader an active searcher after meaning rather than the merely passive recipient of an authorial or narrative 'truth'.

This is true even of some relatively trivial (but nonetheless revealing) details. Near the beginning of chapter 19, for instance, the anonymous narrator is giving a humorously ironic and detached but affectionate account of the effect of the hot weather. In the midst of this a paragraph starts: 'It is the hottest long vacation known for many years. All the young clerks are madly in love, and, according to their various degrees, pine for bliss with the beloved object, at Margate, Ramsgate or Gravesend' (p.314). As the reference to 'degrees' makes clear, part of the humour of the passage relies upon the reader recognising small but significant differences in the social status of the three different towns named. In Dickens's hilarious little tale 'The Tuggs's at Ramsgate' (in *Sketches by Boz*) the *nouveau-riche* Mr Joseph Tuggs suggests that the family should go to Gravesend but 'the idea was unanimously scouted. Gravesend was *low.*' Instead they go to Ramsgate, which it is clear the narrator expects us to believe is only slightly less low. In both this tale and in *Bleak House* we assume that the narrator himself would not holiday in either resort. Yet, when Caddy and Prince marry, the narrating Esther tells us with no hint of irony or disapprobation that they are to honeymoon in Gravesend (p.480); clearly her values are very far from those of the anonymous narrator.

It is not, for example, that what the anonymous narrator tells us about Lady Dedlock is neatly complemented by what Esther tells us. There are tensions and gaps between the two accounts; we do not get a seamless and complete picture of her by joining together the alternative views of her provided by the two narrators. Much the same can be said of the portrayal of Inspector Bucket, about whom we learn rather different things from the two narrators.

It is important to stress that not only is Esther ignorant of the anonymous narrator and his narrative, but the anonymous narrator is – although of course aware of Esther as character – ignorant of Esther's narrative. Thus, for example, when the anonymous narrator first introduces Miss Flite at the start of chapter 11, she is introduced to the reader as if the reader had never met her before – although of course we know Miss Flite from an earlier appearance in Esther's narrative, as well as a very brief, anonymous appearance in chapter 1. And at the start of chapter 66 of the novel the anonymous narrator appears to know only the rumours concerning the scandalous goings-on in the Dedlock household, rather than the detail of Lady Dedlock's flight and death (although the passage is so ironic that the ignorance could be being pretended for ironic effect). It is for reasons such as this that it is highly misleading to refer to the anonymous narrator as omniscient. And this lack of omniscience anywhere in *Bleak House* – either in one or other of the two narratives or in their combined vision – is what makes the reader so morally active. We get no clear, unambiguous moral conclusions at the end of the novel. All of the *plot* mysteries are solved for us by the last page of the work, but their moral implications remain for us to puzzle over.

It seems apparent that the disagreements between different critics concerning the plot of *Bleak House* that I referred to in the Survey can be at least partially explained by asking whether the critics in question see the plot as something isolated from other aspects of the novel, or as an element in an organic whole. If we are merely concerned with 'what happens' we may find the plot lacking (although even so I personally find such a view surprising), but if we relate 'what happens' to other crucial elements in the work – the narrative tensions, the patterns of symbolism and imagery, the thematic repetitions – then we are far less likely to be worried by alleged inadequacies in the plot.

The opening of 'Bleak House'

The opening of *Bleak House* is perhaps the most famous of any of

Dickens's fictional beginnings, and it is worthy of the close attention that literary critics have paid to it. Robert Garis has pointed out that 'even the most casual reader' will tend to read the first pages of a novel with 'a kind of close and alert inspection not unlike the close analysis of literary study' (1967, p.7), and so a close reading of a novel's opening pages is not vulnerable to the objection that it submits part of a literary text to a scrutiny quite unlike that given by the 'common reader'. Moreover, although different readers may bring varied expectations and assumptions to the reading of a literary text, a good reader will have a more open mind during the reading of a novel's opening pages than he or she will have during a reading of a later passage, when all sorts of responses to the text read will have narrowed the range of readerly expectation. So let us turn to the opening of *Bleak House*.

The first word of the novel is 'London' – a word that, in defiance of all the conventional rules of grammar, constitutes a full sentence. The capital city, we are led to suspect, will prove central to the story that follows – but it is quickly confirmed that it is a London with specific characteristics accentuated. It is the London of the law – as the second sentence suggests – and a London of all-embracing physical filth. And these two are, we can surmise, linked: the mud is described as 'accumulating at compound interest' like the money that dominates the novel and the legal profession, and it springs back into our minds when, a few pages further on, the legal gentleman Mr Tangle keeps repeating 'Mlud' (that is, 'My Lord') to the Lord High Chancellor.

Moreover, if we have mud in the first paragraph of the novel we have fog in the next: mud and fog, both dirty, unpleasant things, the products of, in the main, horse excrement and coal smoke in the London of Dickens's time. But, also, both *universalising* things (if I may coin a clumsy term) – as the opening of the novel indicates, no one can escape from either. Whether you are prince or pauper, in the London of *Bleak House* you will walk through mud and breathe fog into your lungs. If we have read Dickens's first novel we may remember that the rascally solicitors in *The Pickwick Papers* were called Dodson and Fogg, and this memory may lead us to suspect that the legal references in the novel's first paragraph and the mention of fog in the second paragraph may turn out to be linked. So they are:

in the fourth paragraph we learn that the fog is densest (and the muddy streets are muddiest) at Temple Bar, and that at the very heart of the fog sits the Lord High Chancellor in his High Court of Chancery.

We are faced, then, with an interesting contrast in these opening paragraphs. On a *grammatical* level everything is disconnected: sentences do not even have verbs, and we are given a set of statement-like phrases with no explicit grammatical indication of the nature of the connection between them. The opening of the novel is almost a list: we are given a succession of things with no relationship between them.

But on a *symbolic* level the impression is different: everything is related, because everything is common. We don't ask what the relationship between the mud and the smoke containing the flakes of soot in it is, because we perceive that both constitute the common lot of all who live in London.

This contrast between disconnection and universal relationship is, I think, a central aspect of *Bleak House*. On the one hand, everything seems so separate, so isolated. But on the other hand everything is related to everything else.

To me, all this suggests that Dickens wanted (at least in terms of his perhaps-unconscious creative insight) the reader to perceive the world of *Bleak House* in terms of surface disconnection and isolation, and underlying unity. Thus, so far as the 'anatomy of society' argument is concerned, my own feeling is that *Bleak House* stands or falls as a portrayal of a *system* rather than as a succession of marvellous but disconnected perceptions – as, for instance, John Carey (1973) argues. Those who suspect that 'close readings' and the detection of 'patterns of imagery and symbolism' are the invention of modern literary critics have, I think, to see how carefully and consistently a novel such as *Bleak House* constructs a vision of interconnections that leads us, inexorably, to a perception of an all-embracing system at work in the novel and in Dickens's England. The association between the mud and the legal profession, for example, is maintained throughout the novel – we have a reference in chapter 10 to 'law and equity, and . . . that kindred mystery, the street mud, which is made of nobody knows what, and collects about us nobody knows whence or how' (p.186) – a rather coy comment as Dickens (or his narrator) must have known very well what the mud was primarily constituted of and where it came from.

Indeed, at the end of chapter 63 of the novel we have an explicit reference to a system, and it comes, revealingly, at the point at which Mr Kenge has explicitly linked the legal system with England.

My dear sir, this is a very great country, a very great country. Its system of equity is a very great system, a very great system. Really, really!   (p.899)

We are a prosperous community, Mr Jarndyce, a very prosperous community. We are a great country, Mr Jarndyce, we are a very great country. This is a great system, Mr Jarndyce, and would you wish a great country to have a little system? Now, really, really!   (p.900)

Of course, it can be argued – as critics such as Robert Garis and John Carey argue – that Dickens *wanted* to give us a picture of an all-embracing social system in *Bleak House*, but that this part of the novel is clumsy, unconvincing and mechanical in contrast to the marvellous isolated perceptions with which *Bleak House* delights us.

I find this unsatisfactory as a view of the novel, for it is precisely when the particular perceptions are linked to a systematising intelligence that relates them to the rest of reality that they are brought to us so powerfully and strikingly in terms of their quirky idiosyncrasy.

Back to the opening paragraph of the novel. Surely the wonderful particularising insights here are so striking because of their cumulative and interlocking force. The paragraph tells us something about the *whole* quality of life in Victorian England and not just of its surface, physical attributes. Little details such as the 'foot passengers, jostling one another's umbrellas' do not just give us a pictorial impression of a nineteenth-century London street scene (although they certainly do do that): they tell us something profound about the nature of the human relationships in nineteenth-century England, with people all bustling around in pursuit of their private interests and concerns but, willy-nilly and even unconsciously, forming part of a systematic and interlocking mode of behaviour as they do so.

We can note, too, how patterns of reference which will amass layers of symbolic force are introduced as early as in this initial paragraph: we have mention of 'a general infection' (albeit of ill temper) and also of 'the death of the sun'. This sunless autumn is to be challenged, shortly, by the 'Summer sun' of Esther and her associated values: within his portrayal of a universally mired system, Dickens leaves room for a battle between conflicting values.

And, given that the opening of the novel presents us with so much filth, we necessarily respond positively to the two characters who are, later on, associated with brooms: Jo and Esther. Dirt has its enemies in the novel – indeed washing and cleaning have an important moral significance in *Bleak House*, from Esther's sweeping of the cobwebs out of the sky to Jarndyce's cold baths and Charley's laundering to support her family.

The first chapter abounds in the establishing of interconnections between seemingly discrete and separate people, events, institutions. The various solicitors in the cause being discussed in Chancery (Jarndyce and Jarndyce, as we shortly learn) have, in two or three cases, inherited the cause from their fathers (p.50); the theme of inheritance, and that of the intermingling of family histories with legal confusion, are thereby linked. And we are told explicitly that the Court of Chancery has its decaying houses and its blighted lands in every shire,

> its worn-out lunatic in every madhouse, and its dead in every churchyard; which has its ruined suitor, with his slipshod heels and threadbare dress, borrowing and begging through the round of every man's acquaintance; which gives to monied might the means abundantly of wearying out the right . . .   (p.51)

Not only does this passage establish connections crucial to the later development of *Bleak House* (between Chancery, decaying houses such as Tom-all-Alone's, lunatics such as Miss Flite, and the dead, such as Captain Hawdon, who will end up in disgusting churchyards), but it also suggests a link between the particular, contemporary reference to social abuses and the larger concern with both Dickens's own systematically organised society and also more universal moral issues. 'Monied might' is simultaneously a reference to those like Tulkinghorn and the Smallweeds who use their financial muscle to exploit and subdue others, and also a more generalised reference to any misuse of the power given by

wealth at any time and in any place. Arguments about whether
Dickens was a contemporary reformer or a moralist concerned
to make generalisations about human good and evil seem to me
to be misleading; he was clearly both, and these two aspects of
his fictional writing depend upon and strengthen each other.

The treatment of Jo, for instance, is surely aimed at what
Dickens saw as a scandalous neglect of children in
contemporary England, but the humanism which informs his
writing here has far more than a local significance and can
easily be responded to by the modern reader. We may feel that
there are few children in our society in the same condition as Jo
(although perhaps we should not be too complacent about
this), but we should know that there are millions of other Jos in
the rest of the world, and Dickens's portrayal of Jo raises
perennial questions regarding our moral responsibility towards
children.

Of course there is some sentimentality in the account of Jo's
death, but much less, I think, than in some of the other, more
notorious, child deaths in Dickens's works. Jo is undoubtedly a
realised character, not a puppet; his life and death affect us both
in terms of this realised individuality and also as representative
of the lives and deaths of real children. We can see from the
contemporary review of *Bleak House* in *Putnam's Magazine* that
Dickens's fellow Englishman could be made to think about
such real lives and deaths as a result of having read the novel
(Dyson, 1969a, p.79). Dickens's musings on Jo's illiteracy and
the uncompromising portrayal of Jo's hounding to death by
Inspector Bucket are tough-minded and direct rather than
sentimental. In contrast to the death of Little Nell (in *The Old
Curiosity Shop*), Jo's death directs our attention to realities rather
than fantastic evasions of reality.

And for the present-day reader of the novel the account of Jo
has more than a historical import: it relates social deprivation
and suffering to larger questions involving the organisation of
society, and it insists upon the humanity of even the most
deprived and uneducated – something that is, alas, never out of
date or redundant.

Crucial to an appreciation of Dickens's genius is the
recognition that he sees nothing in isolation. The linking of Jo's
death to the disease contracted either in Tom-all-Alone's or the
hideous graveyard in which Hawdon is buried – this relates Jo

and his death to the total organisation of society. Disease is such a powerful symbol for Dickens in *Bleak House* because it involves different kinds of expressive connections: it arises from specific, concrete and material living-conditions, living-conditions which are themselves the cause of particular social realities, and it also links the poor with those rich who wish to disclaim any relationship with or responsibility for them. A significant part of the power of *Bleak House* stems from this insistence upon seeing everything (and that includes people) in their historical development and in their interrelationships within an all-embracing social system.

'The System'

Two important points about the novel need to be stressed. First, Dickens really is concerned to portray *a whole society; Bleak House* includes characters from every social class. If this seems a rather unremarkable claim, we need to remind ourselves of how few English novels this can be said. Some four decades after the publication of *Bleak House*, E.M. Forster, in his 'Condition of England' novel *Howards End*, is able to write, 'We are not concerned with the very poor. They are unthinkable, and only to be approached by the statistician or the poet. This story deals with gentlefolk, or with those who are obliged to pretend that they are gentlefolk' (1910, p.58). It is clear that Forster's 'England' is smaller than is Dickens's – smaller in a social and, accordingly, in a moral sense. Thus my phrase 'all-embracing social system' is meant to be understood to be making a serious point. My second point is that part of the pleasure of reading such a novel as *Bleak House* comes from that process of making links, connections, comparisons and parallels to which the novel commits the reader. And the morally important implication of this is that we are encouraged to engage in the same process in our view of the life of society – both Dickens's society and ours.

Dickens does, therefore, portray the workings of a complex *system* in *Bleak House*, a system which destroys the lives of those enmeshed in its mechanisms. But this does not in his view absolve those who operate the system from any moral responsibility for its workings. A crucial section here occurs in chapter 15 of the novel, in which Gridley, on hearing Jarndyce's comment that he (Jarndyce) has been 'unjustly treated by this monstrous system' (p.268), replies at ironic length, pointing out how everyone involved in Chancery washes their hands of moral responsibility for its effects by saying that it is the system that is at fault. Gridley concludes by saying that, even if he does no violence to those who run Chancery in this life, 'I will accuse the individual workers of that system against me, face to face, before the great eternal bar!' (ibid.) Dickens, we must insist, is no determinist: human beings can not shrug off their moral responsibilities onto the workings of an inhuman system – even if (as *Bleak House* surely reveals) he perceives that society *is* systematic in its overall workings, and *does* put pressure on individuals to contribute to evils which they may not personally desire. In such a situation, the novel frequently implies, a failure to inquire about the results of one's actions – or a positive attempt to remain ignorant of them – constitutes the ultimate moral failure of responsibility. The point is made very directly about Chancery and the legal profession, and we can see Guppy and Vholes as representative examples of two sorts of response to the system. Guppy retains a valuable sense of moral responsibility even within his service of the Law, while Vholes uses the Law as an excuse for utterly immoral behaviour.

But the points that are made about the legal system have a clear relevance to society as a whole. Consider Esther's comments in chapter 24 on the Court of Chancery, and see how easily her comments could be applied to society at large, with the administrators of England having the same responsibility for their connivance with the system as have the administrators of Chancery. She describes all Chancery's legal participants 'perfectly at ease, by no means in a hurry, very unconcerned, and extremely comfortable' (p.399), and comments,

> To see everything going on so smoothly, and to think of the roughness of the suitors' lives and deaths; to see all that full dress and ceremony, and to think of the waste, and want, and beggared misery it represented; to consider that, while the sickness of hope deferred was raging in so many hearts, this polite show went calmly on from day to day, and year to year, in such good order and composure; to behold the Lord Chancellor, and the whole array of practitioners under him, looking at one another and at the spectators, as if nobody had ever heard that all over England the name in

which they were assembled was a bitter jest . . . this was so curious and self-contradictory to me, who had no experience of it, that it was at first incredible, and I could not comprehend it. (p.399)

I agree with James M. Brown that we have to understand Chancery in *Bleak House both* as a portrayal of the actual legal institution, and as 'an alien force in itself, a thing with its own life, external to the individuals who have created it – hence, an appropriate symbol for the essential condition of mid-Victorian England' (1982, p.10). (Brown is talking both about Chancery in *Bleak House* and about the Circumlocution Office in *Little Dorrit.)*

But not just mid-Victorian England: the portrayal of Chancery seems to me to condemn any form of social organisation that can run smoothly by subordinating or destroying the humanity of its human components. What is striking in Dickens's works is that, in spite of the fact that he is writing during the heyday of Victorian capitalism, we find in his works no praise at all of the principle of competition, and this fact must qualify Orwell's objection that Dickens never attacks either private enterprise or private property. A powerful speech of Ada's towards the end of chapter 5 describes what are clearly competitive relationships as indistinguishable from being someone's enemy:

I am only grieved that I should be the enemy – as I suppose I am – of a great number of relations and others; and that they should be my enemies – as I suppose they are; and that we should all be ruining one another, without knowing how or why, and be in constant doubt and discord all our lives. It seems very strange, as there must be right somewhere, that an honest judge in real earnest has not been able to find out through all these years where it is. (p.108)

This passage seems to me to be aimed at the heart of the Victorian ideology of success and competition, and to pose against it the need for a social order which is based on co-operation rather than competition and which, rather than discriminating between individuals on the basis of a social hierarchy, accepts that all share a common humanity. In Richard Carstone's progressive alienation from Mr Jarndyce we see enacted the divisive potential contained within the ideology that *Bleak House* implicitly attacks.

Unhappy families

Moreover, Dickens is wonderfully adept at revealing the ways in which forms of social organisation and individual human personality are involved in and constituted by one another. Chancery, we see, ruins many families, but it is based on family rows itself: without dissension between family members it would cease to exist. When Esther and Miss Flite hear about the mysterious woman who has obtained Esther's handkerchief from Jenny, Miss Flite hypothesises that the woman in question is the Lord Chancellor's wife, adding in explanation, 'He's married, you know. And I understand she leads him a terrible life. Throws his lordship's papers into the fire, my dear, if he won't pay the jeweller!' (p.552). The system which destroys families is run by people who belong to unhappy families themselves: the system reproduces itself by means of the miseries it creates.

To move on to discussion of the novel's treatment of the family is again to confront the problem of levels of meaning in *Bleak House*. On the one hand it seems clear that Dickens was directly concerned with the maintenance of what recent feminist writers have called 'gender roles'. When Mrs Jellyby informs us that her public duties are 'a favourite child' to her (p.387), there seems little doubt that Dickens is making the simple point that a mother's 'proper sphere' is that of the household, and that to adopt public duties as a favourite child is to neglect one's real children. This argument is paralleled at a national level: before England turns to the suffering abroad it should look to its own children at home. As Mr Jarndyce remarks in chapter 6 (significantly titled 'Quiet At Home'), 'The universe . . . makes rather an indifferent parent' (p.122); real parents such as Skimpole (to whom Jarndyce is talking) who neglect their parental duties are invariably criticised.

But the reader of *Bleak House* does not generally experience the novel as an essentially conservative tract arguing for the maintenance of traditional domestic roles. The reason for this is surely that there is a tension between different levels of meaning in the novel so far as commentary on the family is concerned. There are occasions on which characters express opinions on the family which are very much in accord with mid-Victorian bourgeois morality: Ada's description, at the end of chapter 60, of her conception of her duty as Richard's wife is a good example: 'when I married Richard, I was quite determined, Esther, if Heaven would help me, never to show him that I grieved for what he did, and so to make him more unhappy. I want him, when he comes home, to find no trouble in my face' (p.880). This is reminiscent of the advice given by Mr Jellyby to Caddy concerning her marriage, and there seems little doubt that it reflects Dickens's conscious beliefs about the role of wives within marriage – the beliefs to which John Stuart Mill took such great exception. Against this we have, however, to set a number of opposing elements in the novel, elements which challenge and undercut the conventional morality of passages such as the above.

Most important of these – and here I agree with T.A. Jackson – is the Bagnet household. This is the happiest and most tension-free of all the families in *Bleak House*, and it is *de facto* run by a woman. That it is *de jure* run by a man intent on preserving the appearance that he is in charge has the important effect of undercutting what Dickens says elsewhere in the novel about gender roles. Now, of course, Mrs Bagnet is not fighting for the vote for women or neglecting her household duties for foreign causes (interestingly, however, Dickens seems to forget that military campaigns abroad are just as much 'causes' as are Mrs Jellyby's charitable interests in Africa). But she is certainly not a wife in the mould of Ada, or of Ada's expressed values. And, just as the conventional roles do not bring happiness to Ada and Richard, neither do they bring happiness to any of the other conventionally organised families in the novel. The Dedlock family is – revealingly – childless, and this sterility seems to stem from Lady Dedlock's lovelessness. Until Sir Leicester is able to display love and magnanimity towards his wife the relationship consists of nothing but show, and in spite of this fact it is not happy. Inspector Bucket wishes the paralysed Sir Leicester 'better' in chapter 56, and hopes that 'these family affairs' will be 'smoothed over – as, Lord! many other family affairs equally has been, and equally will be, to the end of time' (p.820). 'Smoothing over' does not suggest any very encouraging development at the heart of this ultraconventional marriage, although in fact Sir Leicester's behaviour seemingly ends the Dedlock curse, that curse which originated in a quarrel between husband and wife.

Moreover, Dickens's portrayal of the Sir Leicester – Lady
Dedlock – Hawdon relationships is, eventually, without
sentimentality or stereotypical predictability. Most readers
are, surely, surprised and moved by the nature of Sir Leicester's
response to his discovery of Lady Dedlock's infidelity; from
having been something of a caricature, Sir Leicester becomes a
more rounded figure with a convincingly depicted inner life –
an inner life of which we had been given no sign previously. And
in going to Hawdon's grave Lady Dedlock, surely, renounces
that earlier, fatal, renunciation of love and sexuality. *Bleak
House* cannot, I think, be faulted for its portrayal of female
sexuality. Both with Esther and with Lady Dedlock, Dickens
insists upon the right of women to a full and loving sexual life.
We may contrast the portrayal of Volumnia, whose
inadequacies seem to relate both to her dependent status and to
her being single.

But is this Dickens the man laughing at an 'old maid' –
unsympathetic to a woman who does not marry? *Is* the novel
one more suited to male readers, because it presents a view of
the world with a masculine bias? In part, the answer to this has
to be 'yes'; but only in part. Some of the stereotype characters in
the novel – Ada in particular – are clearly related to a masculine
wish-fulfilment view of women. And the puzzling strength of
the Esther–Ada relationship may well be in part a projection of
Dickens's private sexual complexes – the novelist may well be
able to 'love' Ada in proxy through Esther. But, although we
may feel something puzzling about the Esther–Ada relationship, this puzzle may be partly explicable in terms of the
created world of the novel. Given their position in society and
their general subordination to men, women like Esther and Ada
needed strong, perhaps quasi-erotic relationships, with their
equals. And this need could generally be filled only through
relationships with other women. The 'need' behind the
passionate Esther–Ada relationship may be the need of an
insecure, illegitimate and unprivileged woman, or the need of a
woman committed to a disastrous marriage to a man she loves,
rather than the need of a sexually odd male author. Whatever
the case, Esther for me certainly exists. I don't always like her,
and at times I sense that Dickens has not completely solved the
problem of using her as a narrator, but for me she certainly has
a head, a body and an independent life.

Dickens *does* give us a number of recurrent 'types' and recurrent characters in *Bleak House*, but we should remember that a character can *both* be a 'type' *and* have individual qualities. Prince Turveydrop is clearly one of the family of 'feminine men' who inhabit the world of Dickens, but I think that most readers experience him too as a convincing character.

Before we leave the topic of the family, we should perhaps comment upon the links and parallels drawn between the purely domestic families in the novel and the larger 'family' of England. First-time readers of *Bleak House* may well be struck by the way in which Esther is described as a *queen* on a number of occasions. In chapter 36 Esther tells us that she knew she was as innocent of her birth 'as a queen of hers' (p.571), and in chapter 59 this honour is more directly extended to Esther by Inspector Bucket, who adds (perhaps mentally!) a capital letter to the description: '"My dear," he returned, "when a young lady is as mild as she's game, and as game as she's mild, that's all I ask, and more than I expect. She then becomes a Queen, and that's about what you are yourself"' (p.857).

England, we can see clearly, is the largest of the unhappy families in *Bleak House*. The Buffys and Duffys, Doodles and Coodles are obviously neglecting their 'family' responsibilities as fundamentally as are Mrs Jellyby and Mr Turveydrop. Dickens, faced with these neglectful parents, goes to the Queen herself to find a satisfactory symbol for parental duty — although the comparison works both ways, and we may assume that Dickens would also like to see England led by a monarch who would brush some of the cobwebs out of Parliament in the way that Esther does out of Bleak House.

If Esther is described as a queen, Sir Leicester Dedlock is seen as simply honourable, manly and true in his treatment of his wife. And we are told that 'Nothing less worthy can be seen through the lustre of such qualities in the commonest mechanic, nothing less worthy can be seen in the best-born gentleman' (p.851). It would seem, therefore, that in spite of the male-biased and stereotypical elements in *Bleak House* there can also be found what we can refer to as a democratic vein of argument in the novel. The passage quoted above does not, of course, argue that 'the commonest mechanic' should be sitting in Parliament instead of Buffy and Coodle, and when we call Dickens a democrat we should not assume that he supported all forms of legislation aimed at ensuring formal equality before the law for all men – and *Bleak House* makes it quite apparent that he did not want such formal equality for men and women. But there *is*, nonetheless, a democratic humanism in the novel; the reader does get the strong sense that this is a work which does see all human beings – rich and poor, adults and children, men and women – to be possessed of a common humanity. Dickens certainly laughs at William Guppy's class pretensions (Dickens always seems to laugh at those who want to rise socially – to laugh at or disapprove of), but he recognises and celebrates Guppy's humanity. And, as I have already argued, this gives even the present-day reader a sense of the relevance of the novel to our own time.

Humour

Bleak House – like all of Dickens's novels, is funny. It is not his funniest novel by a long chalk, and it is pervaded by a tone of gloom and pessimism that sets the humorous passages in a certain relief. But we cannot talk about the reader's experience of the work without mentioning the central and crucial fact that it makes us laugh. Humour is notoriously difficult to write about: we all know that, while a joke may be funny, the explanation of a joke can be tedious. Critics of Dickens (including myself) are generally wary of trying to say too much about what is such a tricky topic.

But the pleasure that we get when Mr Snagsby, given false confidence by a successful, earlier intervention, suggests in the midstream of Chadband's oratory that the reason we cannot fly is, simply, that we have 'No wings', is not peripheral to our pleasure in reading *Bleak House*. Significantly, the interjection is both very funny and also of serious import. For it cuts through the cant and hypocrisy of Chadband's drivel with a direct perception of the realities of human life of the sort that lies at the heart of Snagsby's revealed worth. Chadband is hateful because his words celebrate his own self-importance and make no contact with human realities outside himself; Mr Snagsby, in contrast, is a morally valuable character because he perceives (all too strongly, so far as his personal comfort is concerned) the human miseries of others such as Jo, miseries need food and clothing and love rather than cruelly irrelevant pieties. All this is, I think, made overt in the reader's mind in the wonderful flash of humour as Mr Snagsby ventures his ill-considered but woefully effective remark. Humour in *Bleak House* is centrally connected to Dickens's – and the reader's – perception of basic human realities.

Thus I agree with John Carey that a crucial aspect of Dickens's humour is his ability to see through pretence (1973, p.54), but disagree with him when he argues that Dickens has no comic method that can express sympathy for the object of his humour, but can yet see its humour (p.76). I think that we do simultaneously laugh at Mr Snagsby and also sympathise with him when he ill-advisedly comments upon our earthbound nature; he is discomfited, but we are laughing more at what this discomfiture reveals (of good in him and bad in Mr Chadband) than at the discomfiture itself.

With this – and perhaps a few other examples – we get as close to laughing out loud as we ever do in *Bleak House*. In general the humour is not of this variety, ranging from the ironic and almost bitter humour of the anonymous narrator to the whimsical humour of, for instance, the wonderful meal that Mr Guppy, Bart Smallweed and Mr Jobling have together in chapter 20. The present reader must in the last resort judge for himself or herself, but for my part I find Dickens neither demanding attention here as the jealous performing artist and social lion, nor slighting the humanity of his characters. Of course it is true that we look at the three dining gentlemen with the anonymous narrator (who at this point is surely very close indeed to Dickens himself in the reader's mind); and it is also true that we laugh *at* the three in different ways on occasions.

Dickens's humour, then, so hard to write about, is so important not only to the enjoyment of such a novel as *Bleak House*, but also to its creation of a set of coherent moral values. The humour enacts and reveals a humanity, the humanity that is always there at points when we feel that the novel is conveying something important. There are certainly negative elements intertwined in Dickens's humour – he was human himself rather than perfect – but we have only to compare him to such a writer as Evelyn Waugh (1903–66) to realise how humane his humour generally is. And, if we are encouraged to feel socially superior to Mr Guppy, we are also humorously encouraged to feel morally superior to Sir Leicester Dedlock early on in the novel. Here we may suspect that Dickens's own complex class position is important; Dickens himself could feel socially superior to the clerk who wanted to rise (he had been such a lawyer's clerk himself) and morally superior to the absurd aristocrat. But, importantly, in neither case can we say that Dickens denies the humanity of the individual concerned; Guppy's selfless warning to Lady Dedlock in chapter 55, and Sir Leicester's magnanimous response to the uncovering of his wife's guilt are sufficient evidence of that.

Character

Let us turn, finally, to the question of Dickens's characters in *Bleak House*. I suggested earlier that (as critics such as Susan Horton have argued) the anonymous narrator's ignorance of, or silence about, the inner lives of certain characters should not be taken to assume that these inner lives are non-existent. This is where the distinction between an omniscient and a merely anonymous narrative voice is very important. We have already seen that there are some things about which the anonymous narrator is ignorant of which we have learned from Esther's narrative; thus just because the anonymous narrator does not know about Tulkinghorn's inner life does not mean that he has none. The anonymous narrator tells us, in chapter 2, that Lady Dedlock is 'childless' (p.56: the words '(who is childless)' were inserted by Dickens at proof stage; see Harvey Peter Sucksmith's commentary [1970, p.336]); either we have to assume that the anonymous narrator is lying here, or that this part of the narrative is not all-knowing. In fact, the anonymous narrator seems to be possessed of ironic detachment and moral insight, but little more factual knowledge than is the common possession of the different social groups with which the novel treats. As critics such as Susan Horton have suggested, because certain crucial areas of ignorance in the information we get from the two narrators parallel areas of ignorance common in everyday social life, the novel forces upon the reader problems analogous to those problems (assessing other people, for example) that we meet in day-to-day living. If we were to know everything about Tulkinghorn then the novel would not make us think about the problems of assessing and living with such characters in real life.

Character and calling

We do, however, know a fair amount about Tulkinghorn. Lady Dedlock tells Esther that Tulkinghorn is indifferent to everything but his calling (p.567), a comment which touches upon a repetitive area of inquiry in *Bleak House*. What is the relationship between 'what we are' and 'what we do' – between, in other words, our personality and our profession? Dickens is responsive to large and significant social changes here; during the eighteenth and nineteenth centuries we can observe a significant shift in the way people are defined and define themselves in Britain. Whereas at the beginning of the eighteenth century what was important was what you were, what station of life you were born to, by the end of the nineteenth century it was perhaps equally important to ask what you did, what job or calling you had.

When, in chapter 6, Coavinses arrests Skimpole for debt, the latter begs him to keep his temper, adding,

> Don't be ruffled by your occupation. We can separate you from your office; we can separate the individual from the pursuit. We are not so prejudiced as to suppose that in private life you are otherwise than a very estimable man, with a great deal of poetry in your nature, of which you may not be conscious.   (p.125)

As it turns out, Skimpole is (unwittingly) quite correct: Coavinses *does* turn out to be an admirable man in private life with regard to the carrying-out of his family responsibilities, but we also learn that his neighbours took a less philosophical view of his work than that professed by Skimpole, blaming the man for his calling (see chapter 15 of the novel). Mrs Blinder tells Mr Jarndyce, who has asked whether Coavinses had any other calling, 'No, sir . . . he was nothing but a follerer' (p.264), and this contrast between a seemingly total devotion to a 'calling', and a private personality apparently very much unsuited to the requirements of this calling, clearly fascinates Dickens.

Lady Dedlock, we may assume from her remark to Esther

about Tulkinghorn's having an indifference to everything but his calling, believes Tulkinghorn to be a man whose private self has been totally overcome by his 'calling'. In fact, as the information we receive from the anonymous narrator suggests, Tulkinghorn is more likely to be a man who uses the cover of his job to indulge secret aspects of his personality which are not related to his professional responsibilities at all. This, surely, is what is suggested by his seeming indecision once he has uncovered the truth about Lady Dedlock; the logic of his preceding search would surely point to the need immediately to reveal all to Sir Leicester. If he really were indifferent to all but his calling, and his calling is to represent Sir Leicester's interests, then he would tell Sir Leicester at once what he has discovered. But to do so would be to lose his ability to exercise power over Lady Dedlock, that exercising which we are clearly meant to perceive brings him such sadistic pleasure. And thus he searches for excuses to do nothing – thus maintaining his ability mentally to torture Lady Dedlock. This – if true – suggests that Tulkinghorn is just as much a portrayal of sexual neurosis as are Esther and Lady Dedlock (if we accept such a view of their depiction).

Mrs Leavis is quite right to insist upon his hatred of women, but it is a hatred that appears to have a strongly sexual element. I mentioned previously the 'double' he is given: the bachelor friend who gives his watch one day to his hairdresser and walks home and hangs himself. To me this is not a hint that Tulkinghorn is homosexual: his obsessive hatred of women in general and Lady Dedlock in particular suggests neurotic heterosexual frustration.

> There are women enough in the world, Mr Tulkinghorn thinks – too many; they are at the bottom of all that goes wrong in it, though, for the matter of that, they create business for lawyers. What would it be to see a woman going by, even though she were going secretly? They are all secret. Mr Tulkinghorn knows that, very well.   (p.276)

Part of Tulkinghorn's desire to unmask Lady Dedlock may be – as is here suggested – jealousy of a rival secrecy to his own. But part seems also to be sexual jealousy: Lady Dedlock has indulged her passion for Hawdon, and Tulkinghorn appears not to be able to accept that for that she shall go unpunished.

His name, of course, has layers of connotative significance:

skulking, primarily perhaps, but 'horn' has sexual meanings, horns are the sign of a cuckold, and 'horn' is slang for penis or erection. Tulkinghorn is also described as 'an Oyster of the old school' (p.182), and, although the primary meaning here is that – like an oyster – he is hard to prise open, it is also worth remembering that the Victorians popularly believed oysters to have aphrodisiac powers.

Tulkinghorn has, then, an inner life; indeed, in spite of the anonymous narrator's professed ignorance of some aspects of it, he does reveal much about it to us – as in the passage I quoted above. And in some ways we can appreciate Mrs Leavis's point that there is less mystery about Tulkinghorn than the critics have suggested: he is a mysterious *man*, but not quite such a mysterious *character*. I don't think that readers generally find Tulkinghorn nearly so puzzling as do critics, although it remains true that the secrecies in his portrayal do force the reader to exercise the sort of active intelligence that real people often require us to use.

Inspector Bucket, however, does puzzle many readers. Once again the relationship between the *man* and the *job* is crucial; arresting George, Bucket says, 'Now, George . . . Duty is duty, and friendship is friendship. I never want the two to clash, if I can help it . . . (p.734). Like Coavinses, Bucket tries to lead a split life. But like Coavinses, he finds it impossible at times. The humanity that leads him to arrest George with such delicacy, and to which Esther bears testimony ('He was really very kind and gentle' she tells us in chapter 57 (p.826) is in sharp contrast to his heartless moving-on of Jo. And Skimpole is surely right that Bucket was more blamable in offering the bribe of five pounds than Skimpole was in taking it. Moreover, in his comments to George about duty and friendship the words 'if I can help it' have an ominous ring; it is clear that, if Inspector Bucket can *not* help it, then it is friendship that will go by the board. The puzzle that Inspector Bucket constitutes for the reader, then, relates to his being split between an essentially decent private self and a potentially heartless 'calling'. And he is thus part of this cumulative inquiry into the relationship between private identity and public work that is so important in *Bleak House*.

We can relate this, yet again, to the anatomy of society, for in anatomising society Dickens also anatomises society-in-people.

This is why it is so revealing that the Lord Chancellor is, as a man, a kind and considerate individual. It is his role and office which are inhuman, not his character and personality (which might even be argued of Vholes, too).

When George journeys north to find his brother he asks a workman whether he knows the name of Rouncewell thereabouts.

> 'Why, master,' quoth the workman, 'do I know my own name?'
> "Tis so well known here, is it, comrade?' asks the trooper.
> 'Rouncewell's? Ah! you're right.'
> 'And where might it be now?' asks the trooper, with a glance before him.
> 'The bank, the factory, or the house?' the workman wants to know. (p.901)

The process whereby a name – the most 'personal' word a person possesses – can become the sign of inanimate institutions and businesses is, Dickens recognises, a very odd one. It was easier for Dickens to recognise the oddity than it is for us, because in Dickens's time the phenomenon was relatively new. But the 'extension' of a name in this manner is not all: what if this extension is into different and even opposed areas? What is the real Rouncewell –a person, a bank, or a factory? And how odd, again, that the workman George meets should talk of 'Rouncewell' as if it were 'my own name'! A name no longer denotes a single, uncomplicated individual: it covers institutions, other people as well. Where does this leave the human identity of George's brother?

'Character' in *Bleak House* is, then, not a matter of how Dickens portrays isolated 'personalities'. It may sometimes seem like this on the surface, but, the more we probe into the novel's characters, the more we realise that Dickens is exploring some fundamental, and historically new, questions about how human identity is formed and expressed.

After his collapse and partial recovery Sir Leicester tells George that 'You are another self to me' (p.849). The comment indicates how Sir Leicester's sense of himself is dependent upon confirmation from outside; as his world collapses he needs external support just to go on being himself. 'You are familiar to me in these strange circumstances, very familiar', Sir Leicester tells George shortly after making the above-quoted comment; George's familiarity helps him to retain a sense of his personal identity, which the shock of recent happenings has threatened to deprive him of.

I have spoken mainly about male characters in the past few pages, because the issue of an identity division between self and job is obviously more relevant to men in a society in which men have jobs in the public world and women do not. But women – the novel shows – have their own forms of division in Victorian society. Esther's desexualised persona as 'Dame Durden', the household angel, is not the whole Esther: there is a passionate individual in Esther that is, eventually, allowed expression in marriage to Woodcourt. And as Ellen Moers (1973) points out, a surprisingly large number of women in *Bleak House* do work: Charley and Hortense, Esther, Mrs Bagnet, Mrs Bucket, Mrs Rouncewell and Caddy Jellyby (and her mother!). In many of these cases we see a tension between the identity that the 'calling' requires or implies, and the inner self that reacts against the work. Moreover, Lady Dedlock too is as much divided as is any other character in the novel – between a public persona as the proud, fashionable, bored aristocratic wife, and the passionate, increasingly desperate secret self. Even Ada conceals aspects of her feelings and thoughts from Richard. In *Bleak House* women's characters are no less complex or subject to socio-historical conditioning than are men's.

But do Dickens's characters ever change or develop – or are those critics who deny this to be conceded a powerful point? The measured depiction of convincing psychological change – such as George Eliot achieves with the characters of Dorothea and Lydgate in *Middlemarch* – is not Dickens's strong point. I have earlier quoted George Orwell's view of this matter, and he repeats, essentially, the view of G.K. Chesterton that Dickens is never successful in describing psychological change; 'his characters are the same yesterday, to-day and for ever' (1906, p.154). But can we square such views with Esther's growth of maturity and confidence in *Bleak House?* Or with Sir Leicester's 'rebirth' after his discovery of his wife's secret history? Or even with Richard Carstone's moral disintegration as the evils of Chancery possess him more and more? In none of these cases, it is true, do we feel that the depiction of psychological change is as masterly as is George Eliot's, but neither is it contemptible.

That we have come back to society and history at the end of a discussion of character in the novel tells us something about

Dickens's organic vision of life in *Bleak House*. No novel shows the interconnectedness of things more convincingly than this one. If everything in *Bleak House* is, directly or indirectly, connected to everything else, then that is because this is how Dickens saw life itself.

References

The following is divided into sections according to the use made of the works in question in the present book, as well as according to the intrinsic qualities of the works themselves. In some instances the same work appears in more than one section.

The date given in textual references is that of the first, or first generally available, edition. Where a later edition is mentioned below it is from this edition that quotations have been taken and to which page references given in the present book refer.

Social and historical studies

Brown, James M., *Dickens: Novelist in the Market-Place* (London, 1982).

Jackson, T.A., *Charles Dickens: The Progress of a Radical* (London, 1937).

Leavis, Q.D., *'Bleak House:* A Chancery World', in F.R. and Q.D. Leavis, *Dickens the Novelist* (London, 1970), pp.118–86.

Miller, J. Hillis, *'Bleak House* and the Moral Life', *Charles Dickens: The World of his Novels* (Cambridge, Mass., 1958); repr. in Dyson (1969a), pp.157–91.

– Introduction to Charles Dickens, *Bleak House*, ed. Norman Page, (Harmondsworth, 1971) pp.11–34.

Orwell, George, 'Charles Dickens', in *Inside the Whale* (London, 1940); repr. in *The Collected Essays, Journalism and Letters of George Orwell*, ed. Sonia Orwell and Ian Angus, vol. I: *An Age Like This* (London, 1968), pp.413–60.

Sanders, Andrew, *Charles Dickens Resurrectionist* (London, 1982).

Shaw, George Bernard, Foreword to the Edinburgh Limited Edition of *Great Expectations* (1937) pp. v–xx; repr. in Wall (1970), pp.284–97.

Smith, Grahame, *Charles Dickens: 'Bleak House'* (London, 1974).

Spilka, Mark, 'Religious Folly', *Dickens and Kafka* (Bloomington, Ind.,

1963); repr. in Dyson (1969a), pp.204–23.

Stoehr, Taylor, *'Bleak House:* The Novel as Dream', *Dickens: The Dreamer's Stance* (Ithaca, NY, 1965); repr. in Dyson (1969a), pp.235–43.

Walder, Dennis, *Dickens and Religion* (London, 1981)

Welsh, Alexander, *The City of Dickens* (Oxford, 1971)

Williams, W.P., 'Of and Concerning "Jarndyce v. Jarndyce"', *The Dickensian*, XLI, (no.273) (Dec 1944), p.27.

Wilson, Edmund, 'Dickens: The Two Scrooges', *The Wound and the Bow* (London, 1941); rev.edn, 1952, pp.1–93.

Studies concerned with narrative method or form

Broderick, James H., and Grant, John E., 'The Identity of Esther Summerson', *Modern Philology*, LV, (no.4) (May 1958), pp.252–8.

Deen, Leonard W., 'Style and Unity in *Bleak House'*, *Criticism*, III (no.3) (Summer 1961), pp.206–18; repr. in Korg (1968), pp.45–57.

Eliot, T.S., 'Wilkie Collins and Dickens', *The Times Literary Supplement*, 4 Aug 1927, pp.408–10; repr. in Wall (1970), pp.278–80.

Forster, E.M., *Aspects of the Novel* (London, 1927; repr. Harmondsworth, 1962).

Friedman, Norman, 'The Shadow and the Sun: Archetypes in *Bleak House'*, *Form and Meaning in Fiction* (Athens, Ga., 1975), pp.359–79; previously published in a different form as 'The Shadow and the Sun: Notes Towards a Reading of *Bleak House'*, *Boston University Studies in English*, III (1957).

Garrett, Peter K., *The Victorian Multiplot Novel* (New Haven, Conn., and London, 1980).

Harvey, W.J., *'Bleak House:* The Double Narrative', *Character and the Novel* (London, 1965), pp. 89–99; repr. and title added in Dyson (1969a), pp.224–34.

Lambert, Mark, *Dickens and the Suspended Quotation* (New Haven, Conn., and London, 1981).

Larson, Janet L., 'The Battle of Biblical Books in Esther's Narrative', *Nineteenth-Century Fiction*, XXXVIII, (no.2), (Sep 1983), pp.131–60.

Miller, J. Hillis, *'Bleak House* and the Moral Life', *Charles Dickens: The World of his Novels* (Cambridge, Mass., 1958); repr. in Dyson (1969a), pp.157–91.

Smith, Grahame, *Charles Dickens: 'Bleak House'* (London, 1974).

Spilka, Mark, 'Religious Folly', *Dickens and Kafka* (Bloomington, Ind.,

1963); repr. in Dyson (1969a), pp.204–23.

Sucksmith, Harvey Peter, *The Narrative Art of Charles Dickens: The Rhetoric of Sympathy and Irony in his Novels* (Oxford, 1970).

Zabel, Morton Dauwen, '*Bleak House:* The Undivided Imagination', first published as the Introduction to the Riverside Edition of *Bleak House* (Boston, Mass., 1956); repr. in Ford and Lane (1961), pp. 325–48.

Feminist studies and studies of Dickens's treatment of women

Barickman, Richard with MacDonald, Susan and Stark, Myra, *Corrupt Relations: Dickens, Thackeray, Trollope, Collins and the Victorian Sexual System* (New York, 1982).

Mill, John Stuart, 'Letter to his Wife, March 1854', repr. in Wall (1970), p.95.

Moers, Ellen, '*Bleak House:* The Agitating Women', *The Dickensian*, LXIX, no.369 (Jan 1973), pp.13–24.

Slater, Michael, *Dickens and Women* (London, 1983).

Studies of Dickens's characters

Broderick, James H., and Grant, John E., 'The Identity of Esther Summerson', *Modern Philology*, LV, no.4 (May 1958), pp.252–8.

Brook, G.L., *The Language of Dickens* (London, 1970).

Dyson, A.E., '*Bleak House:* Esther Better Not Born?' (1969b), in Dyson (1969a).

Leavis, Q.D., '*Bleak House:* A Chancery World', in F.R. and Q.D. Leavis, *Dickens the Novelist* (London, 1970), pp.118–86.

Major, Gwen, '*Bleak House* on the Air', *The Dickensian*, XLI, no.273 (Dec 1944), pp.65–7.

Miller, J. Hillis, '*Bleak House* and the Moral Life', *Charles Dickens: The World of his Novels* (Cambridge, Mass., 1958); repr. in Dyson (1969a) pp.157–91.

Scott, P.J.M., *Reality and Comic Confidence in Charles Dickens* (London, 1979).

Smith, Grahame, *Charles Dickens: 'Bleak House'* (London, 1974).

Wilson, Angus, 'Charles Dickens: A Haunting', *Critical Quarterly*, II, no.2 (Summer 1960), pp.101–8; repr. in Ford and Lane (1961), pp.374–85.

'Reader-response' critics and studies of Dickens's readers

Daleski, H.M., *Dickens and the Art of Analogy* (London, 1970).

Friedman, Norman, 'The Shadow and the Sun: Archetypes in *Bleak House*', *Form and Meaning in Fiction* (Athens, Ga., 1975), pp.359–79; previously published in a different form as 'The Shadow and the Sun: Notes Towards a Reading of *Bleak House*', *Boston University Studies in English*, III (1957).

Horton, Susan R , *The Reader in the Dickens World* (London, 1981).

Leavis, Q.D., *'Bleak House: A Chancery World'*, in F.R. and Q.D. Leavis, *Dickens the Novelist* (London, 1970), pp.118–86.

Scott, P.J.M., *Reality and Comic Confidence in Dickens* (London, 1979).

Biographical studies, and critical studies based upon a thesis about Dickens the man

Carey, John, *The Violent Effigy: A Study in Dickens' Imagination* (London, 1973).

Chesterton, G.K., *Charles Dickens* (London, 1906).

Forster, John, *The Life of Charles Dickens* (London, 1872–4): new augmented edn with notes and an index by A.J. Hoppé, two vols (London, 1966).

Garis, Robert, *The Dickens Theatre: A Reassessment of the Novels* (Oxford, 1965).

Johnson, Edgar, *Charles Dickens: His Tragedy and Triumph*, two vols (New York, 1952); ch on *Bleak House* repr. in Dyson (1969a), pp. 135–56.

Lambert, Mark, *Dickens and the Suspended Quotation* (New Haven, Conn., and London, 1981).

Anthologies of criticism and studies of Dickens's critical reception

Dyson, A.E. (ed.) *Charles Dickens: 'Bleak House'. A Casebook* (London, 1969a).

Ford, George H., *Dickens and his Readers: Aspects of Novel Criticism since 1836* (New York, 1955); new edn (New York 1965).

Ford, George H., and Lane, Lauriat (eds), *The Dickens Critics* (New York, 1961).

Korg, Jacob (ed.) *Twentieth Century Interpretations of 'Bleak House'* (Englewood Cliffs, NJ, 1968).

Wall, Stephen (ed.) *Charles Dickens: A Critical Anthology* (Harmondsworth, 1970)

Also cited in text

Forster, E.M. *Howards End* (London, 1910; repr. Harmondsworth, 1975).

Further Reading

Dickens and 'Bleak House'

As this book should have made clear, the *Casebook* on *Bleak House* is a most useful collection of material on the novel which spans a wide historical period. It is edited by A.E. Dyson (1969a). Edgar Johnson's modern biography of Dickens (1952), and John Forster's contemporary one (1872–4) are both excellent and readable accounts of Dickens's life which are, in many ways, complementary. Journals such as *Victorian Studies*, *Nineteenth-Century Fiction*, *Dickens Studies* and *The Dickensian* regularly publish relevant material on the writer and his works. *The Dickensian* in particular is a mine of useful and fascinating material, compulsive reading for library-browsers! An index is available: Frank T. Dunn, *A Cumulative Analytical Index to 'The Dickensian' 1905–1974* (Hassocks, 1975).

Narrative

Two helpful introductory works are Shlomith Rimmon-Kenan, *Narrative Fiction: Contemporary Poetics* (London, 1983), and Tzvetan Todorov, *Introduction to Poetics,* tr. Richard Howard (Brighton, 1981).

Reader-response theory

An essay which points out the many dangers of criticism of the novel which ignores the reading-experience is Ian Gregor, 'Criticism as an Individual Activity: The Approach Through Reading', in *Contemporary Criticism,* ed. Malcolm Bradbury and David Palmer (London, 1970). A recent collection of critical essays on 'reader-response criticism' is *The Reader in the Text: Essays on Audience and Interpretation,* ed. Susan R. Suleiman and Inge Crossman (Princeton, NJ, 1980).

Critical theory

Among the many books on criticism and critical theory are *Modern Literary Theory: A Comparative Introduction,* ed. Ann Jefferson and David Robey (London, 1982); Terry Eagleton, *Literary Theory: An Introduction* (Oxford, 1983); and *Criticism and Critical Theory,* ed. Jeremy Hawthorn (London, 1984).

Index

Index

Characters from *Bleak House* are given in italics.